GW00674536

TONY MERIDA
RUTH
FOR YOU

thegoodbook
COMPANY

Ruth For You

© Tony Merida, 2020

Published by:
The Good Book Company

thegoodbook.com | www.thegoodbook.co.uk
thegoodbook.com.au | thegoodbook.co.nz | thegoodbook.co.in

ISBN: 9781784983987

Printed in Turkey

Cover design by Ben Woodcraft

CONTENTS

Series Preface   5

Introduction   7

1. The Sojourn *Ruth 1:1-5*   13

2. The Return *Ruth 1:6-18*   29

3. The Arrival *Ruth 1:19-22*   45

4. The Field *Ruth 2:1-13*   61

5. The Meal *Ruth 2:14-23*   77

6. The Threshing Floor *Ruth 3:1-18*   93

7. The City Gate *Ruth 4:1-12*   107

8. The Son *Ruth 4:13-22*   121

Glossary   135

Bibliography   141

SERIES PREFACE

Each volume of the *God's Word For You* series takes you to the heart of a book of the Bible, and applies its truths to your heart.

The central aim of each title is to be:

- Bible centered
- Christ glorifying
- Relevantly applied
- Easily readable

You can use *Ruth For You:*

To read. You can simply read from cover to cover, as a book that explains and explores the themes, encouragements and challenges of this part of Scripture.

To feed. You can work through this book as part of your own personal regular devotions, or use it alongside a sermon or Bible-study series at your church. Each chapter is divided into two (or occasionally three) shorter sections, with questions for reflection at the end of each.

To lead. You can use this as a resource to help you teach God's word to others, both in small-group and whole-church settings. You'll find tricky verses or concepts explained using ordinary language, and helpful themes and illustrations along with suggested applications.

These books are not commentaries. They assume no understanding of the original Bible languages, nor a high level of biblical knowledge. Verse references are marked in **bold** so that you can refer to them easily. Any words that are used rarely or differently in everyday language outside the church are marked in gray when they first appear, and are explained in a glossary toward the back. There, you'll also find details of resources you can use alongside this one, in both personal and church life.

Our prayer is that as you read, you'll be struck not by the contents of this book, but by the book it's helping you open up; and that you'll praise not the author of this book, but the One he is pointing you to.

Carl Laferton, Series Editor

INTRODUCTION TO RUTH

Recently when I announced that we were going to study *Ruth** as our church's Advent series, several people cheered! We are not an overly expressive church, and so this vocal celebration struck me. Why are Bible readers so drawn to the book of *Ruth*?

For starters, *Ruth* is one of the best short stories ever written. Who doesn't love a good story? "Once upon a time" and "They all lived happily ever after" are phrases cherished by many. *Ruth* possesses all the elements of a well-written story. We are drawn to the *characters*: grieving Naomi, loyal Ruth, and compassionate Boaz. The *setting* is also intriguing. It takes place during the time of the judges (Ruth 1:1); and the locations include Bethlehem, **Moab****, Boaz's field, a threshing floor, a city gate, and a bedroom. The *plot* involves a story of **redemption** which, as we learn, is part of the grand story of redemption (4:17-20). Naomi stands in the middle of the *conflict* of the book, as a widow with no son to carry on the family's line. At the heart of the *resolution* is Boaz, a figure who shows a lot of similarities to David's greatest son, Jesus.

The love story between Ruth and Boaz is remarkable. Like many love stories through the years, two unlikely people unite. Think of other stories you know: a young woman and a terrifying monster in *Beauty and the Beast*; a failed nun and a military captain in *The Sound of Music*; a roughneck cowboy and a classy nurse in *Open Range*; a stager and an Irish innkeeper in *Leap Year*; and a human and a vampire in *Twilight*! If you like these sorts of stories, then welcome to *Ruth*. Here, two very unlikely people get together—an Israelite gentleman and a Moabite widow—and she ends up being one of the many-times-great-grandmothers of Jesus.

---

* For the purposes of clarity and conciseness, I have chosen to italicize "Ruth" when referring to the book of Ruth, as opposed to the character Ruth, which will remain un-italicized.

** Words in **gray** are defined in the Glossary (page 135).

At first glance, the title "Ruth" may come as a bit of a surprise. She is a Moabite! This is the only Old Testament book named after a non-Israelite. That she was a Moabite makes it even more surprising, as Moab was a long-standing enemy of Israel. Further, Ruth speaks less than Boaz and Naomi, and the speeches she does make are shorter than those of the other two characters.

We could call the book "Naomi" instead—she is the one who loses everything within the first few verses and who gains a wonderful recompense in an unexpected way at the end of the story. The main tension of the plot comes from her sense of abandonment by God in contrast to the way God uses her family to provide a king for Israel. Or we could give this book the title "Boaz"—he is the one who speaks the most words and who brings resolution by marrying Ruth and providing security for the future. Or, based on the importance of a child, Obed—the son born to Ruth and Boaz at the end of the story—could bear the title. But I would submit that "Ruth" does indeed make the most sense. She is present in every scene, except for the city-gate scene in chapter 4, and it is through Ruth's actions that Naomi's crisis will be resolved. Ruth is the one who brings all the characters, and the whole plot, together.

Why Study Ruth?

As well as the fact that it's a beautifully written love story, there are many other reasons to study *Ruth*.

First, *we need to study it because it is God's word.* Paul tells us that all of Scripture is "profitable" (2 Timothy 3:16, NIV), and that includes the book of *Ruth*. While *Ruth* may be like several popular love stories, it is most certainly unlike them all in this regard: it is "God-breathed" Scripture. We, the people of God, do not live by bread alone, but by every word that proceeds from the mouth of God (Matthew 4:4), and therefore we need the book of *Ruth* for our own spiritual nourishment.

Second, *we need to see the larger story of God's redeeming grace.* God has given us his whole word—all 66 books—as one large story.

The Bible begins as a story—"In the beginning, God created the heavens and the earth" (Genesis 1:1)—and it ends as a story in the book of Revelation, albeit with a surprising type of ending (for the end is a new beginning!). The Bible does not come to us as a **systematic theology** book, as important as these books are. Theology books are written topically and aim to explain various **doctrines**. But the Bible is a story, and all its little stories fit into the larger story. The Bible really is a unified book of **redemptive history**, of which Jesus is the hero. We therefore need to study individual stories on their own, while keeping the big picture in mind, in order to discern how the little story contributes to this overarching story. *Ruth* advances the story of God's redeeming grace to Adam's **fallen** race. It magnifies God's *hesed*—his **covenantal faithfulness** and unceasing kindness.

Third, *we need a greater appreciation of God's **providence***. We have real-life details of real-life situations in the lives of real-life characters. To paraphrase the hip hop group Beautiful Eulogy, most of us live in the book of *Ruth*, not in the book of Exodus! That is, we do not gather **manna** from heaven every morning and walk through parted seas. We live by faith in God's "ordinary providence." There are no miracles in *Ruth*, but that does not mean God is inactive. We must never assume that a lack of miracles means God is not at work. He is present in the lives of these seemingly insignificant characters, displaying his meticulous providence, just as he is at work in our own lives. Our God is working out all things according to the counsel of his will (Ephesians 1:11), and he is worthy of our trust and adoration.

Fourth, *we need to remember God's global mercy.* The **gospel** is not for Jewish people only but for the whole world, including Moabites like Ruth. God not only allows Ruth to become part of his people but actually uses her as a vital part of his plan. He brings this non-Israelite right into the heart of his people and gives her a place of honor. We need to remember this. Reading *Ruth* should help us to understand and reflect God's heart for the nations in our own lives and ministries.

Finally, *we need models of genuine godliness*. Many Old Testament characters provide us with examples for godly living, and such is the case here. Ruth inspires us to be loyal, sincere, gracious, courageous, and devoted. Boaz gives us a model of manhood: justice-pursuing and not passive, compassionate and not abusive. Naomi's story engenders hope in us, as she goes from emptiness to fullness in the narrative. We are thus instructed and encouraged by what has been written in these former times (Romans 15:4).

I would like to put Daniel I. Block's excellent outline of *Ruth* before you, from his book *Judges, Ruth* (page 587):

- Act 1: The Crisis for the Royal Line (1:1-21)

- Act 2: The Ray of Hope for the Royal Line (1:22– 2:23)

- Act 3: The Complication for the Royal Line (3:1-18)

- Act 4: The Rescue of the Line (4:1-7)

- Epilogue (4:18-22)

Block's outline reminds us of the heart of the narrative. *Ruth is about the coming **Messiah***. This is not just any story about a woman finding a husband or a widow finding a family. We find out at the end of the book that Ruth's descendants will be kings of Israel. She is part of the royal line that eventually leads to Jesus.

To help us step through the story scene by scene, I have arranged this commentary around various locations and movements in the narrative:

1. The sojourn

2. The return

3. The arrival

4. The field

5. The meal

6. The threshing floor

7. The city gate

8. The son

I am indebted to scholars like Block, as well as other **commentators** that I have consulted: Robert Hubbard, K. Lawson Younger Jr., Iain M. Duguid, Sinclair Ferguson, and Peter Lau and Gregory Goswell. I have tried to cite each scholar with integrity. I do not claim to be a scholar but a reflective practitioner, and I am grateful for scholars who work tirelessly to bless the Lord's church by giving us such wonderful resources.

1. THE SOJOURN

Certain words are devastating. No one wants to hear the words "We're going to have to let you go" from their employer, or "Brace for impact" from a pilot, or "I'm sorry, but there's nothing more we can do" from a doctor.

Ruth opens with some devastating words. The first time I read the opening five verses of *Ruth* to my children and explained the names of the characters and a bit of the background, they were shocked and perplexed. Things go from bad to worse.

Coming after the book of Judges, which displays the problems of Israel on a broader national and local level, *Ruth* zooms in on one particular family's trials and tragedies. It takes place during the time in which "the judges ruled" (**v 1***), which was a period of spiritual darkness. We also read of a "famine" in the land, likely a sign of judgment. And things get even worse, as we read of three funerals. Within a few verses we are left with a grieving widow in a foreign land, with her two widowed daughters-in-law (v 2-5).

We live in the same fallen world as these women and can relate to these hardships to some extent. But the immediate suffering of this family is not the only thing we need to notice. The central focus of *Ruth* actually concerns the origins of Israel's royal line. The genealogy that appears at the end of *Ruth* clarifies this point (4:18-22). The crisis introduced here at the start of chapter 1 involves the widowhood of Naomi and Ruth, meaning the family line is threatened. But the genealogy shows us that Obed, whose birth resolves the crisis and continues the family line, will be the grandfather of David, Israel's greatest king. God

---

* All Ruth verse references being looked at in each chapter part are in **bold**.

has promised to send a king to Israel to rule on God's behalf (Genesis 17:6; 35:11; 49:10; Numbers 24:17; Deuteronomy 17:14-20). In Judges, this is threatened because of widespread unfaithfulness. In *Ruth*, that threat begins to be lifted.

There is a hint at all of this in *Ruth* **1:1**, as we read of Elimelech's "Ephrathite" lineage. This was a name for those whose families were from Bethlehem. The book's first readers might have known that David was of this line—a link we read about in 1 Samuel 17:12.

When the Judges Ruled

The book of *Ruth* takes place during one of the darkest periods in Israel's history: the days of the judges. The period of the judges came after the land was settled and before the monarchy was established. During this time there was no national government. Israel was a collection of tribes. These judges were local "chieftains" that were called to overthrow foreign oppressors. They were local military leaders, not national political leaders.

The book of Judges shows the downward spiral of Israel's national and spiritual life, and underlines the need for a godly king to lead the people (Judges 2:11-19). A repeated cycle of events occurs: God's people rebel against him; God gives them into the hands of their oppressors; God's people repent (at least during the first few cycles); God sends a deliverer to give the people a period of rest. Tim Keller's *Judges For You* contains a helpful diagram of these cycles (page 207). The final chapters of Judges (Judges 17 – 21) stand outside this downward spiral and show in graphic detail a nation that has totally lost its way, becoming every bit as bad as the **pagan** nations of the day.

We are not told where exactly *Ruth* fits in the season of the judges. What we do know is that the author of *Ruth* sees this whole period as something in the past. The way some of the customs in *Ruth* are explained by the author suggests that the book was written a considerable time after the completion of the story (for example, Ruth 4:7). *Ruth* was written either during Israel's monarchy or during the post-exilic period. It is looking back on a bygone age. This means that we can see the whole period of the judges as a backdrop for reading *Ruth*.

It was a period filled with violence, idolatry, moral depravity, and civil war. The following words are repeated in the book of Judges and are the final line we read in the book: "There was no king in Israel. Everyone did what was right in his own eyes" (Judges 21:25; see also 17:6; 18:1; 19:1). It is against this black backdrop that Boaz and Ruth shine. It is somewhat surprising to find godly examples in this time period! Further, it is in this dark season that the providence of God shines. Despite sin and rebellion, God is working out his redemptive purposes.

Could not that description—"everyone did what was right in his own eyes" (Judges 21:25)—be given to your context as well? False religion, biblical ignorance, political corruption and disgrace, civil war, and violence surround us. In many places today, people extol the virtue of "tolerance" above all other virtues. Their version of tolerance could be summed up by the same phrase from Judges—everyone doing what is right in his or her own eyes. Those who hold to it often have a negative reaction to the truths of Scripture, especially to what the Bible says about sin.

But this problem is not just outside the church. Adopting the prevailing worldview in today's culture is a temptation for the church as well. When certain sins are normalized in the culture, it is tempting to tolerate them in the church. Many churches have caved in to cultural pressure and discarded certain ethical teachings that the Bible presents clearly. Many Christians lack the boldness to withstand these temptations; others lack the theological discernment to detect such errors.

It is in this kind of context that Christians are called to shine. Ruth and Boaz inspire us to do so. The nobility and courage of Ruth and the compassion and righteousness of Boaz will dazzle us. When we see their actions in the context of the judges, then it motivates us to go against the customs of our own day and follow Christ instead.

A Godly Character

There is another way in which understanding the context of *Ruth* within Scripture helps us to focus on the godly character displayed by Ruth and Boaz. The Christian **canonical order** places *Ruth* after Judges, showing the historical flow of things. However, in some He-brew traditions it is placed after Proverbs, and in others it is placed before Psalms. Daniel I. Block explains:

> "In the vast majority of Hebrew manuscripts and published edi-tions, Ruth appears as the first of five Megilloth, the five scrolls regularly read at annual Jewish festivals. In the Ben Asher fam-ily of manuscripts, this group as a whole appears after Proverbs … The arrangement in the majority of Hebrew manuscripts, however, contradicts the order of books in several Talmudic lists, most notably Bava Batra 14b, which places Ruth ahead of Psalms at the beginning of the Writings."
>
> (*Judges, Ruth*, page 589)

Proverbs ends with chapter 31, extolling the marks of a wise and vir-tuous woman. It is an **alphabetic acrostic** of 22 lines celebrating a worthy woman. If you have never read Proverbs 31, now would be a good time to go read it. Reading *Ruth* alongside this chapter allows us to see an example of what a Proverbs 31 woman looks like in an ungodly culture.

The similarities between Proverbs 31 and *Ruth* are notable. In their book *Unceasing Kindness* (page 42), Peter Lau and Gregory Goswell note the following:

- Both women are energetic and active (Proverbs 31:15, 27; Ruth 2:2, 7, 17).

- Both work to supply the needs of their households (Proverbs 31:15, 21; Ruth 2:18).

- Both show kindness (*hesed*; Proverbs 31:26; Ruth 3:10).

- Both are praised as superior by their husbands and by others (Proverbs 31:28-29; Ruth 3:10-11; 4:15).

- Both work hard (Proverbs 31:13, 27; Ruth 2:2, 17, 23).

- Both fear God (Proverbs 31:30; Ruth 1:16; 2:12).

There are differences, too, including those of their class and race, but these similarities are present.

Ruth does not have all these virtues at the beginning of the book. She has yet to confess faith in **Yahweh** and become integrated into the Israelite community. This is an important point: it is not possible to live a truly godly life without a relationship with God! He is the One who forgives sin and transforms us into holy people. But here is also a word of hope, as God is still in the business of turning pagans into godly **saints**.

> God is in the business of turning pagans into saints.

Other Hebrew traditions, meanwhile, place *Ruth* just before the Psalms. This makes sense: the sweet psalmist of Israel was David, Ruth's great-grandson. He was the king God provided through Ruth. He was the one the tribes of Israel were so in need of.

The rule of David had its ups and downs, and he was by no means a perfect king—God's people would have to wait until the coming of Jesus for that. But David was a godly man. Almost as soon as we hear about him, we are told that the Lord was with him (1 Samuel 16:13), and we are shown that he trusted the Lord (17:37). His psalms also show what he was like, both as a follower of God and as a leader: he prays for blessing for his people (Psalm 3:8), he cries out for justice for them (7:7-9), he calls them to turn to God (51:13), and he leads them to praise him (145:6). David's confidence and delight in the Lord are completely different from the brokenness and immorality we see in the book of Judges, when Israel had no king.

As we read the book of *Ruth,* we will see that Ruth's godliness is crucial to the plot. In particular, Boaz admires her devotion to her mother-in-law (Ruth 2:11-12), and this apparently leads him to protect her. God uses Ruth's characteristics of diligence and loyalty to provide for her and for Naomi. He works through Ruth's godly attitude and, through her descendants, ultimately provides a king to lead his people into godly ways. Ruth, then, gives Christian women a model to follow. She is a surprising contrast with the immoral times in which she lives: "when the judges ruled" (**1:1**).

For us, too, having a godly character provides a way in which God can work through us. Following Ruth's example is not about taking the moral high ground. It is about "bearing fruit" (John 15:5; Galatians 5:16-24); as we remain devoted to Christ, the Holy Spirit works in us to produce good works. Godly living is how we show ourselves to be Christ's disciples and bring glory to him.

Questions for reflection

1. Can you think of some examples of the people you know doing what's right in their own eyes—both in and out of church?

2. How does it help to consider the book of Ruth beside the books of Proverbs and Psalms? Does it make you approach it differently?

3. What do you most hope to learn about or grow in as you read *Ruth*?

PART TWO

Famine and Faithlessness

The "famine in the land" (Ruth **1:1**) highlights the economic challenges of the day. People were hungry and destitute. Interestingly, the famine even reached Bethlehem (which means "house of bread"). Israel was supposed to be the land flowing with milk and honey (Exodus 3:8), but you could not even find bread in the house of bread!

We have to read this situation with Deuteronomy in mind. God promised blessing on his people for obedience, which included things like defeating their enemies and productive crops (Deuteronomy 28:1-14). But God warned them of curses for disobedience, which included infertility, defeat, and famine (28:15-68; see also 1 Kings 16:29-34; 17:1). Due to Israel's disobedience, during the time of *Ruth*, God's warning came true. The fields were barren, and the crops failed. The barns were empty. People were desperate because they were under the judgment of God. At the same time, we should remember that historically God had used famine to deliver his people and advance his **sovereign** purposes (for example, Genesis 45:5-8).

This famine should have led the people to repent. God promised that he would lift the curse, should they do so (Deuteronomy 30:2-3, 8-10). But as we read of one particular family, led by a man named Elimelech, we see that instead of repenting, he takes matters into his own hands (Ruth **1:2**). Elimelech, whose name means "My God is King," does not act as if his God is King. Sinclair Ferguson says, "Instead of turning back to the Lord, this little family turn their backs on the Lord, and go to live in Moab" (*Faithful God*, page 24). Instead of mourning over the sin of the land and asking God to restore things, Elimelech leaves the fields of Bethlehem for the fields of Moab.

We can certainly sympathize with a man wanting to provide for his family. But this was a unique situation. This was the promised land. Elimelech's move was not like that of a person today migrating to another country out of desperation, seeking opportunity. God had promised that his presence would dwell in Israel. God had promised to bless his people there, should they walk in his ways.

Elimelech's journey at first appeared to be a quick "drive thru," a brief "sojourn" (Ruth **1:1**). But then he and his family "remained" (or "settled") there (**v 2**), and Naomi ended up living in Moab for ten years (**v 4**). Elimelech acted like the people of the day. He did what was right in his own eyes. The appropriate response to the famine would have been to remain in Israel, to repent, to call others to repent, and to trust God. But it seems he felt more at home in the land of compromise than the land of promise.

Elimelech took with him his wife, Naomi, whose name means "pleasant" or "sweet." (People in the southern part of the United States might call her "Sweetie Pie"!) He also took his two sons, Mahlon and Chilion. The name Mahlon is likely derived from a word meaning "sick." The name Chilion denotes "frailty and mortality". Block contends that these names were probably not given by their parents but are signs, preparing the readers for what is about to happen to them and to Naomi (*The King Is Coming*, page 68).

Moab, which lay on the other side of the Dead Sea, was an interesting choice of destination. The Moabites traced their origin back to the incestuous relationship between **Lot** and his oldest daughter (Genesis 19:30-38). Later a king of Moab, Balak, had hired the prophet Balaam to curse Israel, and the Moabite people had begun to seduce Israelites into sin by inviting them to participate in false worship and sexual immorality. As a result, the Lord slew 24,000 Israelites (Numbers 25:9). Most recently Moab's King Eglon had oppressed Israel (Judges 3.14). In going to Moab, Elimelech and his family were certainly turning their back on the Lord and his people.

Going God's Way

Elimelech's decision stands as a warning to us. We must not do whatever is right in our own eyes. We must not make decisions without reference to God and his word.

The longer I have pastored, the more I have observed how many professing Christians do not really believe that the Bible is enough. They do not really believe it is sufficient for life and godliness (2 Peter 1:3; 2 Timothy 3:17). For example, some pragmatic Christians live by whatever makes the most practical sense. Sometimes this is good, but often what is deemed "practical" may not be biblical or God-honoring. So whenever the Bible says one thing and their own reason says another, the former is quietly ignored or explained away, and the latter wins out. Others base major decisions on their feelings and their experiences. They may use the phrase "God told me" to justify a decision, sometimes when that decision clearly violates the clear teaching of Scripture (like marrying an unbeliever)! But God is not going to tell anyone to do something that violates his word.

When people do consult Scripture, they often do so without a proper approach to biblical interpretation and application. I recently heard of a church member who had said this to a pastor friend of mine: "God told me to move to Israel in 2012." When my friend asked him how he knew, the man opened the Bible and showed him Genesis 12. He said, "See, God told Abraham to move to the promised land in chapter 12. And it's on page 20 in my Bible. I put it together, and I believe God is saying to me, 'Move to Israel in 2012.'" Sadly, this man was serious. This may sound ridiculous to us—and it is. But it is the kind of thing that happens all the time. I have heard many similar stories, such as that of a woman seeing a cloud shaped like a "J," and then concluding that she was to marry "James."

We do not need to do tricks with the Bible, look for letters in the sky, or expect God's will to be spelled out in our cereal. We may need to do what is unpopular and challenging, not what is most practical and easy.

We should see Elimelech's decision as a warning. He did not listen to his own name; he did not treat God as his King. Faithful Christianity means seeking to live by the word of God in biblical community, among Spirit-filled, prayerful, wise saints. This is the pattern for good decision-making—not going our own way, as Elimelech did.

Death and Despair

We might compare Elimelech's situation with that of **Jacob**, who also fled from famine. Interestingly, he and his family flourished in exile—since, crucially, he fled with God's blessing (Genesis 46:1-19). But Elimelech and his sons do not flourish. Instead, things get worse. In Moab, Naomi experiences a nightmare: a triple bereavement. Her husband, Elimelech, dies first (Ruth **1:3**). We are not told why or how. All we are told is that Naomi is left with her two sons.

These two sons marry Moabite women, Orpah and Ruth. 4:10 reveals that Ruth was the wife of Mahlon, while Orpah married Chilion.

The author does not evaluate the brothers' decision to marry Moabite women. The law did not prohibit marriage to Moabites specifically (Deuteronomy 7:3-4), but marriage to them was discouraged based upon the spirit of the law. Block says, "The Moabites are not listed with these **Canaanite nations**, but since they were the people of Chemosh, a foreign God, the spirit of the law would have them included" (*Judges, Ruth*, page 629).

Further, Deuteronomy 23:3-6 prohibited Moabite offspring from entering the assembly until the tenth generation—in other words, forever. (This does not mean that those who converted to the faith of Israel and joined the people of Israel by doing so could not enter in. These verses in Deuteronomy underline the "set-apartness" of Israel and God's call to his people to be holy—utterly different from those nations around them. To welcome into the assembly of Israel a Moabite who was still worshiping Moab's gods and following Moab's resistance to the rule and law of Yahweh would have "represented in a most graphic way a violation of the principle of holiness and purity that must characterize Israel in its status as a chosen people" (Eugene H. Merrill, *Deuteronomy*, page 308).)

A sign of Mahlon and Chilion's rejection of God can be seen in their lack of fertility. Neither has children. Yet as soon as Ruth marries Boaz, she conceives. K. Lawson Younger explains:

"The covenantal implications are clear: as Yahweh withheld the rain and produced the famine, so he withheld fertility, hence no children (Deuteronomy 28:4; 18; [compare] 1 Samuel 2:5-6)."

(*Judges/Ruth*, page 412)

This sad introduction ends by telling us of Naomi's gloomy state (Ruth **1:5**). It is easy to imagine her grief as she attends funeral after funeral. Picture her. She is a widow in a foreign land. She has no significance. She has no husband to protect and provide for her. She has no sons—so she has no social standing and no hope of carrying on her family line. She is aging. It is a hopeless situation.

Many know the pain of Naomi. We may experience it through heart attacks, hurricanes, or car accidents; through betrayal, violence, or loss. In this fallen world, we will face suffering. We will weep like Naomi. We will stand beside graves. We may even fear for our lives and wonder how God will provide for our needs. We can identify with Naomi. And we can identify with what Naomi needed: hope.

Hope in Suffering

What do we make of all this tragedy in the opening five verses? We need some help to understand and deal with suffering. Not all suffering is alike, and not all suffering carries the same kind of pain. But this much is true: every single person will suffer.

One of the most encouraging things about the Bible is that it does not hesitate to address suffering. The Bible is a real-life book. If you have some objection to Christianity because of suffering, please notice that the Bible is not silent about this issue. There is not room here for more than a brief overview, but the truth is that every book of the Bible talks about suffering in some way.

The book of Genesis tells us how suffering and death entered the world: because of sin (Genesis 2 – 3). After reading about many types of suffering in Genesis (especially the suffering of Joseph in Genesis 37 – 50), we read about God's people suffering in Egypt (Exodus 1 – 2). In the **Pentateuch**, God's people are given good laws so that they will suffer less. Deuteronomy is about how people suffer in the wilderness, which prepares them for the promised land. The Bible's history books tell us about the suffering of Israel; sometimes it is on account of their own sin and sometimes as a result of the sin of others. The wisdom literature (Job, Psalms, Proverbs, Ecclesiastes, and Song of Solomon) reflects on suffering deeply. The prophets repeatedly address suffering and look ahead to Israel's future Messiah, the suffering Servant (Isaiah 53). Throughout the New Testament we hear about suffering. Finally, the book of Revelation gives us hope in suffering, as we wait for the day in which Jesus will wipe away every tear from our eyes (Revelation 21:4).

So in many ways, we cannot understand Scripture if we ignore suffering. We cannot understand what it means to be human without taking suffering into account. We cannot understand what Jesus endured for us if we do not think rightly about suffering. We will not long for glory if we ignore or dismiss suffering. We cannot understand people, nor will we minister well to hurting people, if we do not understand their suffering, enter into their grief, and walk with them through their pain. And we will not appreciate the sovereignty and faithfulness of God as we ought if we do not think rightly about suffering. For if there is one lesson we learn about suffering in Scripture, it is that it is not outside the control of our sovereign God. The book of *Ruth* magnifies this truth: you can trust him even in suffering. You may be perplexed, but you can trust him.

> We cannot understand Scripture or long for glory if we ignore suffering.

Naomi did not know how things would turn out, but readers have the privilege of knowing her whole story. It is a story that goes from emptiness to fullness, from tragedy to glory. It shows us that God is still trustworthy in the midst of emptiness and difficulty. The question for us is: can we bring ourselves to trust him? Can we still worship and obey God in suffering?

All suffering is painful, but as God's people we must remember that while we will have trouble in this world, we are not alone (John 16:33). By faith in Christ, we have a relationship with God and we have the Holy Spirit, our Comforter, dwelling in us. We have a Savior who is not detached but sympathizes with us in suffering (Hebrews 4:14-16). Jesus knows suffering, not only because he knows all things in a general sense but because he was himself the man of sorrows (Isaiah 53:3). Our Father cares for us and is aware of our needs.

We need more than modern technology and self-help books to deal with our grief. We need the just King, Jesus Christ. The Bible tells us how suffering came into the world, what kinds of suffering we will experience, and what our King has done and will do to make all things new.

Therefore, in suffering we must not turn from our God but to him. We must cast all our cares upon him, knowing that he cares for us (1 Peter 5:7). We must not be shy about "lamenting" to God—a third of the psalms are laments, and it is good and right to pour out our hearts to God in suffering. It is right to sing songs with the community of faith in suffering because, as Christians, we know that glory will soon come. Do not stop gathering with God's people; as we hear the word and participate in the **sacraments**, we are reminded in word and sign that suffering is under God's control, and that there is the hope of glory in the end.

In the next section (Ruth 1:6-22) Naomi will make the decision to return to Bethlehem. This fertile little location just five miles south of Jerusalem was a seemingly insignificant town in the grand scheme of things. But of course it is associated with David (1 Samuel 20:6) and the birth of Jesus (Matthew 2:1; Luke 2:4; John 7:42). In Bethlehem, shepherds would be summoned to come and see the Messiah (Luke 2:8-21). Jesus would be born in the house of bread and would declare himself to be the bread of life (John 6:35). Only in Jesus can we find ultimate satisfaction and eternal life. From Naomi's seemingly insignificant family, in an insignificant little town, would come the Savior of the world, the King of kings (Micah 5:2).

At this stage in *Ruth*, we have not yet heard how Naomi will respond to the loss of her husband and sons. But in this book we will learn the same lesson of hope that we see throughout Scripture. During Naomi's time of darkness, God is working out his sovereign and saving purposes.

We do not always understand what God is doing. But God is at work in the details of our lives. He reigns over all things and is accomplishing his sovereign purposes. I cannot read the story of Naomi without thinking of a favorite hymn, written by William Cowper, which extols the mysterious providence of God:

God moves in a mysterious way
His wonders to perform;
He plants his footsteps in the sea
And rides upon the storm.

Ye fearful saints, fresh courage take;
The clouds ye so much dread
Are big with mercy and shall break
In blessings on your head.

His purposes will ripen fast,
Unfolding ev'ry hour;
The bud may have a bitter taste,
But sweet will be the flower.

Blind unbelief is sure to err
And scan his works in vain;
God is his own interpreter,
And he will make it plain.

Questions for reflection

1. In what situations do you find it hard to follow what the Bible says? How could you speak up for a biblical way of living?

2. Who do you know who needs hope? Why? How could you help them?

3. What experience do you have of God using the sorrows of life for a good purpose? How does that make a difference to how you see the coming week, month and year?

2. THE RETURN

The next portion of *Ruth* presents us with three women—Naomi, Ruth, and Orpah—and the crucial decision they face.

We read first of God's gracious provision to his people (Ruth **1:6**): the famine is over. A decision must then be made. Should they return to Bethlehem? Indeed, the key word in this section is the word "return." This Hebrew word appears twelve times in this single chapter—sometimes translated "turn back," "go back," or "bring back."

Have you ever faced a turning point, a crossroads? In this passage, a geographical and spiritual turning point exists; for the story is not merely about turning back to Bethlehem, but also about turning back to the Lord in faith.

God's Gracious Provision

For the first time in the book of *Ruth*, we now read of good news: Naomi "had heard in the fields of Moab that the LORD had visited his people and given them food" (**v 6**). Covenant blessings have returned in the land of promise. God has "visited" (that is, comforted) his people with food! Upon hearing this news, Naomi decides to return home. It has now been at least ten years since she arrived in Moab. But something happens in her heart that makes her want to go back to Israel.

Grace abounds in every word of this little verse. First, Naomi "heard" of this good news, even while she was "in the fields of Moab." How could she have heard of this change? She had no television, radio, or social media! Somehow the word made its way to the distant fields of Moab, and Naomi responded. The news must have been like water to a thirsty soul (see Proverbs 25:25). The word "heard" is a sign of gracious provision.

Second, it was "the LORD" who provided this remarkable gift of grace. This is the first mention of God in *Ruth*. He is doing what he does regularly in Scripture: providing. There are many examples of this in the Psalms, which are filled with praises reflecting on God's remarkable provision. Ruth's great-grandson King David writes:

"The eyes of all look to you,
  and you give them their food in due season.
You open your hand;
  you satisfy the desire of every living thing." (Psalm 145:15-16)

The Lord worked out his providential and redemptive purposes in just the same way here in *Ruth*. At this bleak time in history, God opened his hand and provided food for the hungry.

Third, grace is expressed in the word "visit." Sometimes this word is used with reference to God's judgment, but here refers to God visiting in blessing. Similarly, throughout redemptive history, this word is used to speak of God's gracious intervention in a crisis. In Genesis 21:1 and 1 Samuel 2:21, the same word is used to speak of God visiting infertile women, enabling them to conceive and give birth. Interestingly, the book of Ruth also involves a story about barrenness and the Lord's gracious intervention. In Ruth 1:6, he visits with food; soon he will visit with fertility.

This is the nature of our God. He intervenes in a crisis. The book of James states that true religion involves "visiting" orphans and widows in their affliction (James 1:27). This means that we are to intervene in the lives of the powerless and voiceless, and come to their aid. Visiting those in affliction is one way we can reflect the nature of God in this broken world, and each of us should seek to do so.

Perhaps God is giving you a burden for orphans. How might you come to their aid? Or maybe you are beginning to grow concerned for the enslaved. Do you have any desire to act on behalf of the elderly, the widowed, or the homeless? What about those who are refugees in your area? We cannot do it all, but we can all do something on behalf of the vulnerable in society.

And why should we do this? Because God has visited us in our affliction! According to the gospel, it is all of us who are the afflicted, the weak and wounded, the sick and sore. And Jesus has come to our aid. Christians are the people who should most identify with the orphan and widow. We were the orphan, and God adopted us. We were the widow, and Jesus became our Bridegroom. We were the stranger, and God made us citizens of heaven. We were the poor, and Jesus gave us a glorious inheritance. We must remember how God has visited us with grace. The proper response is to look out for those who are vulnerable and to visit them with grace ourselves.

> We were the orphan, and God adopted us. We were the stranger, and God made us citizens of heaven.

Fourth, we see grace in the phrase "his people." The language reflects God's covenantal relationship with them: the agreement that he would be their God, and they would be his people (Exodus 6:7). The fertile land is a statement: God has not forgotten Israel. While we do not hear of any acts of repentance, it appears that the good crops in Bethlehem are the Lord's response to genuine **piety** in people like Boaz (Deuteronomy 7:12-15; 11:13-15). Whatever the case, God is mercifully acting on behalf of his people.

One theme in the Bible that is often overlooked, especially in individualistic cultures, is the concept of community. Yet it is a theme woven throughout. God has always purposed to have a people for himself. He displays his glory to his people in providence and redemption, and he displays his glory through his people in their words and deeds. Our faith is personal, but it is not individualistic. In the New Testament, Titus reminds us that Jesus gave himself to redeem us and "to purify for himself a people for his own possession who are zealous for good works" (Titus 2:14). We must not forget that we are saved into a community. The church is not a building we frequent or an event we attend, but a people to whom we belong. We are called to share our lives, to weep together, to pray together, to bear one another's burdens, to study together, and to live on mission together. Never lose the wonder of being part of the people of God, for "once you were not a people, but now you are God's people" (1 Peter 2:10a). This is what we glimpse in this phrase in Ruth **1:6**: "his people."

Finally, we see what God provides for his people: "food." We may be able to list many ways in which God provides and many things to be thankful for, but we should not forget that he is also the One who provides for our most basic needs. This is a consistent concern of God in Scripture. In Genesis, he sent **Joseph** to Egypt in order to preserve the world, especially his own people, from starvation (Genesis 45:5-8; 50:20). In Exodus, he repeatedly sent food and water to the Israelites (Exodus 15:25; 16:13-16; 17:5-6). God's servants **Elijah** and **Elisha** saw the provision of bread for one widow (1 Kings 17:12-15), oil for another (2 Kings 4:2-7), and food for a hundred men in famine (4:38-44). Jesus turned water into wine (John 2:1-11) and fed thousands of people with a few loaves of bread (John 6:5-13). He told his disciples to ask for "daily bread" (Luke 11:3) and not to worry about food or clothing because "your Father knows that you need them" (Luke 12:30).

In modern suburban and urban settings, God's gracious provision for our basic needs is often overlooked. If you live in a place where you frequent a marketplace or a supermarket to purchase food, then you should regularly thank God for his gracious provision. We should be thankful grocery shoppers! The pastor Alistair Begg says, "God stocks the shelves" ("Can this be Naomi?" www.truthforlife.org, accessed September 5th, 2019). Of course, we know that there are farmers, computers, transportation services, and employees that cause those shelves to be filled with food; but there is something very right about this statement. Ultimately it is the Lord who opens his hand and satisfies the desire of every living thing. We must not forget this.

This simple verse contains many hints about the nature of the wonderful provision of our God. He allowed Naomi to hear the news from Israel; he came compassionately to visit those suffering in famine; he came to his people, with whom he had made a covenant; and he did not overlook their basic needs but gave them food. This was the context in which Naomi, Ruth, and Orpah had to decide what to do next.

Back to Bethlehem?

In response to God's gracious provision, Naomi sets out with Ruth and Orpah to return the land of **Judah**. This key word in the chapter, "return," appears in both Ruth **1:6** and **verse 7**. Naomi is an Israelite, so she is returning home. But the other two women are Moabites. For them, it will not be a return trip but a move to a new homeland. Will they go with their mother-in-law?

Conversations dominate the book of *Ruth*, with 56 of the 85 verses consisting of dialogue. There are three conversations that appear in verses 8-18. In **verses 8-10**, Naomi addresses both Ruth and Orpah. In verses 11-14, we see another discussion with all three women involved, including a description of Ruth's and Orpah's brief responses. In verses 15-18, Orpah drops out of the discussion. Naomi and Ruth dialogue, and there we find Ruth's decision to go with Naomi. Lying at the heart of this decision is Ruth's commitment to Yahweh and his people.

Remember, Naomi has bonded with Ruth and Orpah. They have shared a common life together. They have wept at funerals together. They have laughed together. And now, Naomi is returning. We might wonder what is in her head as she makes this decision. She is returning differently than the way she left. She is a widow. How will she be treated? Will people care for her or scoff at her? She has lived in Moab, of all places, for ten years!

Somewhere along the journey, an important conversation takes place. It is a turning point, perhaps at a stop for water or during an overnight stay. Even though she loves these daughters, she feels the need to show some "tough love." She tries to persuade them both to return to Moab. Interestingly, she does not tell them to return to their "father's house," but their "mother's house" (**v 8**), a rare phrase that only occurs three other times in the Old Testament, in contexts involving love and marriage (Genesis 24:28; Song of Songs 3:4; 8:2). Here also, marriage is in view. In the following verses, Naomi specifically refers to them finding a husband in Moab.

Naomi then offers a prayer for the women. She first says, "May the LORD deal kindly with you, as you have dealt with the dead and with me" (Ruth **1:8b**). The word "kindly" is the rich Hebrew word *hesed*, which refers to God's faithful love. It speaks of his loyalty, faithfulness, grace, mercy, and compassion. She wishes for Yahweh to be merciful to them in the midst of harsh circumstances. She believes that God is indeed kind, and that his power and grace extend beyond the borders of Israel. This is her hope: that Yahweh will show them *hesed*. These daughters-in-law have been compassionate to Naomi, and so she longs for them to be richly blessed.

She adds to this prayer by saying, "The LORD grant that you may find rest, each of you in the house of her husband!" (**v 9a**). The kindness from God that she longs for in **verse 8** is now given concrete expression in **verse 9**: rest and a husband. She prays for them to be settled and secure, and for Yahweh to bless them with another husband. She recognizes that such blessings are granted by God as a gift of grace. Will Yahweh be pleased to bless Ruth and Orpah with another husband? The plot thickens.

Immediately after offering these prayer requests, Naomi shows affection, kissing the women, which then triggers much weeping. We can only imagine the emotion here. The language denotes loud crying and mourning. This makes sense. They have spent all this time together, and agonized through trial after trial; to contemplate not seeing each other again would have made anyone burst out into audible lament. After a later exchange, the same language is used again in verse 14, underlining the emotion in this conversation.

Ruth and Orpah initially object to Naomi's wishes, saying, "No, we will return with you to your people" (**v 10**). We are not told why. They could have had many reasons. They may have simply wanted to stay together, knowing the challenges of life that awaited each of them. They surely were concerned for Naomi, an older widow, as well. What is most striking is the reference to "your people." They express a desire not only to go with their mother-in-law but to go to her people. That meant severing ties with the Moabites and joining with a different group. They were, in other words, more attached to Naomi than to their own ethnic people. This idea would seem extraordinary to many now, but it was even more extraordinary in the ancient world. It underlines the depth of devotion they had to each other.

This devotion is another hint at God's provision. Naomi compares the way Ruth and Orpah have treated her with the way she hopes God may treat them: "kindly" (**v 8**). They are reflecting God's *hesed*, his faithful kindness. Naomi is acknowledging the general fact that God is kind. But she does not recognise God's gracious and abundant provision to her and to his people. In the following verses we will see just how bitter she feels toward God.

Questions for reflection

1. What could you do practically to help yourself to see the provision of God in the small details of life?

2. What recent provisions are you thankful for?

3. Whose words do you think are more surprising—Naomi's or Ruth's and Orpah's? Why?

PART TWO

Go Home!

After hearing Ruth and Orpah protest, Naomi makes her longest speech in the book. At this point she remains committed to her proposal that they return to their own homes. She challenges them in the form of questions, first asking why they want to go with her and then asking, "Have I yet sons in my womb that they may become your husbands?" (**v 11**). Her opinion is firm. Without giving her daughters-in-law a chance to respond, Naomi continues her argument. She advises them to "turn back" and "go your way," telling them to be realistic: "I am too old to have a husband" (**v 12a**). She is underscoring her hopelessness; she cannot bear sons as new husbands for them (**v 12b-13a**). She is saying, in effect, *Think it through, ladies. Even if I were to have sons in my old age (which I can't!), you would need to wait years before you could marry them. It's not going to happen. So go back to Moab, where you will have the prospect of another husband. You are better off there!* Implicit in Naomi's statement is the desire for her daughters-in-law to remarry, and not so much for the preservation of her family line. It was customary for a childless widow to marry her husband's brother in order to raise children and continue the dead family husband's line. But Naomi's two dead sons have no brothers, so there is no hope of that happening.

Naomi next adds another firm statement, saying, "No, my daughters" (**v 13b**). That is, *Absolutely not! Do not come with me.* Naomi is surrendering her daughters-in-law to what she is sure will be a brighter future. She explains her perspective: "It is exceedingly bitter to me for your sake that the hand of the LORD has gone out against me." This is a bitter lament. She is wounded, and she shifts her focus from the young women to an accusation against God. She believes that the Almighty's hand has gone out against her, as if she is his enemy. So why go with her? Things could get worse!

Even though Naomi sees God as responsible for her losses and does not interpret things entirely correctly, it is important to note that she does at least see God's involvement in her life. Remember, Naomi has already prayed for her daughters-in-law, asking that God might grant them rest and a husband (v 9). She knows that things are not outside of God's sovereign control. Robert Hubbard Jr. suggests that "bitter complaint cloaked firm faith" (*The Book of Ruth*, page 116).

After first rejecting Naomi's proposal, Ruth and Orpah now face a decision. It is much like considering the cost of discipleship that we are told of in the New Testament (for example, Mark 10:17-31; Luke 9:57-62). Will they forsake all and follow Naomi, or turn back to Moab?

After more weeping, Orpah makes the decision to turn back (Ruth **1:14-15**). She concludes that the safer and more sensible route is to return to Moab, where she may find a husband. She kisses her mother-in-law goodbye and then drops off the pages of Scripture.

Ruth, however, clings tightly to her mother-in-law. The expression carries the idea of deep loyalty, like that of a marriage (see Genesis 2:24). It involves leaving membership of one group and joining another. She has counted the cost and is abandoning everything to journey with Naomi. She will go and live among Naomi's people, although she is not one of them, as Iain Duguid points out:

"There was nothing **kosher** about Ruth. She knew she would be about as welcome in Bethlehem as a ham sandwich at a **bar mitzvah**." (*Esther & Ruth*, page 142)

Yet she clung to her mother-in-law in faith.

Ruth is a picture of risk-taking faith. Her decision to go with Naomi is rooted in her trust in Yahweh, as Ruth **1:16** goes on to highlight. Orpah's decision makes sense on a practical level. But Ruth's decision requires something more than conventional wisdom; it requires faith—the kind of faith we should imitate. It is the kind of faith that bears fruit. It is a relational faith, an active faith.

Your God, My God

Ruth's faith shines in the next few verses. Naomi tries to get her to consider Orpah's decision and do likewise: "See, your sister-in-law has gone back to her people and to her gods; return after your sister-in-law" (**v 15**). We can imagine her even pointing to Orpah, saying, *Look, she's going back. It's the right decision. You should follow her.* The husband argument did not work, so Naomi now opts for the use of peer pressure!

But there is more than peer pressure here. She also mentions "her people" and "her gods." Naomi is reminding Ruth of her religious and national roots. She is urging her to go back to the Moabite way of life and worship.

In this crucial moment of decision, we read of Ruth's stunning profession of faith. Every phrase is worth considering:

"But Ruth said, 'Do not urge me to leave you or to return from
following you. For where you go I will go, and where you lodge
I will lodge. Your people shall be my people, and your God my
God. Where you die I will die, and there will I be buried. May the
LORD do so to me and more also if anything but death parts me
from you.'" (**v 16-17**)

Ruth's statement is well-known due to its poetic power. Ruth is not merely expressing devotion to Naomi; she is expressing faith in Yahweh. Sinclair Ferguson paraphrases Ruth's response:

"Listen! I have been converted. Stop urging me to go back; did
you hear me? I have been converted." (*Faithful God*, page 33)

The center point of the statement is the most important: "Your people shall be my people, and your God my God." The poetic structure of these verses frames this glorious profession of faith. There are five sentences, with this sentence at the heart of what Ruth says.

"Do not urge me to leave you or to return from following you.
For where you go I will go, and where you lodge I will lodge.
Your people shall be my people, and your God my God.

Where you die I will die, and there will I be buried.
May the LORD do so to me and more also if anything but death parts me from you."

The first sentence (**v 16a**) and the fifth sentence (**v 17b**) belong together. The first sentence includes an introductory command, "Do not urge me…" and the fifth sentence is a concluding oath, "May the Lord do so to me…"

The second sentence (**v 16b**) and the fourth sentence (**v 17a**) also belong together. They are a verbal pair: "where you go … I will go, and where you lodge I will lodge" and "where you die I will die, and there will I be buried," showing Ruth's commitment to live and die in the land of Naomi. In the ancient world, there was an association between the local deity you worshiped and the place where you were buried. You had to be buried in the right place to have a restful afterlife. So being willing to die in the land of Israel was, for Ruth, a major sign of her commitment to Yahweh.

In the middle of these two pairs of sentences is the profession of faith: "Your people shall be my people, and your God my God" (**v 16c**). This Hebrew **chiastic** structure accentuates Ruth's calculated response to Naomi.

Ruth has counted the cost, and she is following Yahweh and joining his people. The Hebrew literally reads like this: "Your God, my God. Your people, my people." Ruth is not pledging something in the future but stating something that she has already done: a faith and identity that she already has. She is saying, *Naomi, because your God is my God, and your people are my people, I will go with you.* Ruth's declaration is not primarily about her commitment to Naomi. It is about her commitment to Yahweh. She is saying, *Naomi, the reason I belong to you is because I belong to Yahweh.*

Her statement is similar to the statement we read when God made his covenant with his people Israel: "And I will walk among you and will be your God, and you shall be my people" (Leviticus 26:12; see also Genesis 17:7-8; Exodus 6:7). Ruth is declaring that the God who made a covenant with Abraham, the God who brought his people out of Egypt, is her God too.

Ruth's conversion is confirmed in the next chapter, where Boaz makes this prayer about her: "The LORD repay you for what you have done, and a full reward be given you by the LORD, the God of Israel, under whose wings you have come to take refuge!" (Ruth 2:12). He recognizes her faith. Finding shelter "under ... wings" is used in the Psalms as a statement of personal trust in the Lord (Psalm 17:8; 36:7; 57:1; 61:4; 63:7; 91:4).

> Authentic Christianity involves turning your back on the gods of this world in order to have Christ.

Her conversion is similar to what Paul says of the Thessalonians: "You turned to God from idols to serve the living and true God" (1 Thessalonians 1:9). This is authentic Christianity. It involves turning your back on the gods of this world, and everything else, in order to have Christ.

Orpah takes the broad road; Ruth takes the narrow road (Matthew 7:13-14). Ruth sells everything she has to gain a treasure, the pearl of great price—Yahweh (Matthew 13:44-46).

Naomi gets the message, and in response to Ruth's passionate profession she does not give an answer. She does not say, *Wonderful! Let's go to Bethlehem!* She is just silent (Ruth **1:18**). Often this passage is quoted in marriage ceremonies, but few couples include Naomi's silence! It doesn't have the enthusiastic tone we would like. But whether this silence is hard and begrudging or whether Naomi is simply tired of arguing, she accepts Ruth's decision. They turn for Bethlehem (v 19).

What We Learn from Ruth's Conversion

Here are five lessons that we can draw from this remarkable conversion of Ruth.

First, the conversion of Ruth is one of the primary answers to the problem of darkness in chapter 1. Ruth will be the conduit through whom God pours his grace to the bitter old widow, Naomi. Ruth supports her, and together with Boaz she will provide a new family for her. On a larger scale, for the struggling nation, Israel, Ruth will be the means through whom the nation's greatest king, her great-grandson David, will come. And on the largest scale of all, for a world separated from God and lost in idolatry, Ruth's family line will lead to the Messiah, Jesus Christ, who will come to be the Savior of both Jews and **Gentiles**. We need to see how pivotal her conversion is, not only in her own immediate context, but also in the context of the greater redemptive storyline. When times are dark, God is still at work—and it may take generations, even centuries, to see the full glory of what he is doing.

Second, we can each see our own story in Ruth's. Her transformation should encourage us and fill us with praise toward God. We, too, were once outsiders, but God has made us insiders. We, too, were dead in sin, alienated from God, but in Christ Jesus we have been brought into a relationship with God (Ephesians 2:1-22). We, too, worshiped the gods of this world, but we have turned to the living God! How wondrous is the gospel!

Third, we see the relationship between personal faith and the community of faith in Ruth's conversion. The phrase "my people" emphasizes the fact that individuals are saved into a people. We must all come to faith personally, but that personal faith expresses itself in a community. Sometimes that community of faith is difficult to love—just look at who Ruth was with! Bitter Naomi was probably not an easy or encouraging traveling companion. But God's purpose is to have a people for himself, not just a collection of individuals. It is a privilege to be part of the people of God, despite the challenges that may come in sharing life with them, and it is one of the primary ways by which the world will know we belong to Jesus—by our love for one another (John 13:35).

Fourth, we should never underestimate what God may do through one true conversion. Granted, Ruth is a special case since she is in the family that would become the royal line; but it is often just one conversion in a family or a church that sparks a glorious gospel movement. One conversion often leads to multiple conversions! Sometimes it is through the conversion of just one person that a church is reawakened to the power of the gospel. Sometimes it is just one new believer who brings renewal to long-time saints.

Finally, Ruth's conversion should motivate the church to mission. God still converts outsiders! Ruth, like **Rahab**, who was also an outsider (see Joshua 2:10), heard somehow of the mighty deeds of the Lord, and the Lord brought her to faith. She had lived with Naomi for ten years; while Naomi does not appear to have been a winsome witness, it is clear that somewhere along the way Ruth heard of and believed in the God of Israel, by his grace. Would you pray that God would use you to lead a Ruth to faith? Pray that you may "walk in wisdom toward outsiders," speaking winsome and gracious words, and that he would use you to bear witness (Colossians 4:2-6). In many parts of the world, God is bringing the nations to us! This is the case where I live—people from other nations are literally down the street from our church building. We often have people among us who have never attended a church service before. We must pray that God would use us to lead more "Ruths" to faith.

And what about your own position before God? Have you come to faith in Jesus Christ, the faithful One, who left heaven for earth in order that we may be God's people? Which road will you take: the broad road of Orpah or the narrow road of Ruth? Though none go with you, will you still follow Jesus? Do you think he is worth it?

In his talk, "From a Foreigner to King Jesus" (www.tgc.org), Alistair Begg tells the story of when he was at a café one morning in Cambridge, Massachusetts. He was sitting down reading the Bible and looking over his notes for an upcoming sermon. There was virtually no one in the shop at the time. Then a Chinese student from Harvard entered. Seeing his Bible, she asked if Begg was a Christian, and he said, "Yes, I am." The young student responded, "I am a Christian too." Begg asked, "How did you become a Christian in China?" And she replied, "I entered through the narrow gate." Whoever we are and wherever we are from and whatever lies behind us, there is only one way to Jesus and to life.

That is what happened in Ruth's life. She entered through the narrow gate, and no one who passes through there ever has cause to regret following Jesus Christ. Though he does not promise that life will be easy, he does promise to be with us and satisfy us with his presence forever.

Questions for reflection

1. Do you think Naomi is right to say what she says in verses 11-13?

2. What Ruth-like outsiders could you ask God to lead to faith?

3. How could you show the same risk-taking faith and loyalty to God and his people that Ruth shows in verses 16-17?

3. THE ARRIVAL

Ruth 1 ends as it begins—by talking about bread. It begins with a mention of a "famine" in Bethlehem ("the house of bread," Ruth 1:1), and it ends with mention of the beginning of the "barley harvest" in Bethlehem (**v 22**). This change of circumstances is owing to God's intervention: he "visited his people," providing them with food (v 6).

There are some similarities between Naomi's return and the story of the prodigal son (Luke 15:11-32). In rebellion, the son turned his back on his father and left for a "far country" (v 13). There, he squandered everything, spending all his money, satisfying his sinful lusts. Then there was a "famine" in the land (v 14). Not able to find work, he ends up working with pigs, and was so desperate that he longed to be fed with pig food himself (v 15-16). He was in great need, with no friends and totally alone. Then, Jesus says, "he came to himself" (v 17). He wakes up to the reality that in his father's house is "more than enough bread" to satisfy even the servants of the house. So the son wisely says, "I will arise and go to my father" (v 18a).

Naomi also returns home at the prospect of bread. But the big difference is that, unlike the prodigal son, she does not return broken and contrite. She expresses bitterness instead of brokenness.

Entering the town with Naomi is Ruth, the converted Moabite and loyal daughter-in-law. However, we do not hear Ruth speak in this particular scene. The focus is on the women in Bethlehem, and Naomi's frustration.

The Buzz

We are not given any details about the rest of the rugged road from Moab to Bethlehem. We are just told that they "went on until they came to Bethlehem" (Ruth **1:19a**). But remember that after Ruth expressed her faith in Yahweh and her commitment to Naomi, the reaction was not what we might have expected—Naomi said nothing in response to Ruth. Was the entire trip like that?

However awkward their relationship, the trip would certainly have been physically challenging and, no doubt, emotionally exhausting. Memories of the years they had spent in Moab would surely have flooded their minds. Ruth had spent her whole life in Moab—imagine the emotions that were filling her heart as she left! In particular, they were leaving behind their loved one, Orpah. Naomi now also must have felt the angst of returning to the place where she once lived. Her heart would have been filled not only with memories of the past but also with concerns about the present and the future. She was returning quite differently than how she left.

If you have ever lived in a small town, or in a part of the city that has a tightly knit community, then you can understand what we read next. In places like these, everyone knows everyone. Outsiders are detected immediately, and word spreads fast through the town at the sound of any news or gossip. So "the whole town was stirred because of them. And the women said, 'Is this Naomi?'" (**v 19b**). Naomi shows up unannounced after ten years away, and her presence creates a stir in the town.

This buzz in the town, translated "stirred" (or "excited," NLT, CSB), derives from a word meaning "to throw into disorder, to confuse." The image is of animated conversation in the town. The people of Bethlehem are all talking to one another. The women ask, "Is this Naomi?"

Perhaps their disbelief is founded on excitement; they are full of joy at seeing Naomi again. Or maybe they are judgmental and smug, comparing their own newfound prosperity with her unhappiness—

Looks like Naomi got her comeuppance for leaving Israel! It is also possible that the women of the town have heard of all that she has been through and are concerned for her. Perhaps they sympathize with her and pity her.

Whatever their tone, they can hardly believe that this is the woman they once knew. Naomi has changed. No doubt she has changed physically after ten years. Physical appearance—hair color, weight change, a lined face—is one of the first things we notice in a person that we have not seen in years. We might say to an old friend, "You haven't aged a bit!" Or we may not mention what we really think of their appearance if the aging process hasn't been kind!

But there was more to the change in Naomi than the aging we would expect. The women probably asked this question because of her expression too. Naomi was a woman filled with sorrow. She had left as the "pleasant one" but returned grief-stricken. Naomi had left in her prime, and she returned old and destitute.

Naomi had also changed relationally. She had left Bethlehem with a husband and two sons. She returned accompanied by no men and with a widowed Moabite. Interestingly, the narrator does not tell us that the women said anything about Ruth. The emphasis is on Naomi. They do not say, *Who are these two women?* Are they intentionally avoiding questions about Naomi's companion? Are they embarrassed? The presence of Ruth may have been the subject of private conversations later.

The Bitterness

You have to admire the transparency and candor of Naomi. She responds to this buzz with a sharp response: "Do not call me Naomi; call me Mara, for the Almighty has dealt very bitterly with me" (**v 20**). *Don't call me Sweetie Pie; call me Bitter Woman!* She believes her situation demands a new name—one that reflects her frustration. "Mara" means "bitter," and she insists they call her by that name.

The name "Mara" has a noteworthy history. When God's people rebelled in the wilderness, complaining about a lack of provision, Mara was the name of the place where they grumbled against him (Exodus 15:22-24). This is the same chapter in Exodus that begins with the people singing praises to God for delivering them from Egyptian tyranny through the parting of the Red Sea (v 1-21)! They had come out of slavery, but their hearts were not fully free. So when they could not drink the water at Mara because it was bitter, they murmured. They cried out to the Lord, and he miraculously made the water drinkable and sweet. Naomi here reflects the heart of her ancestors: she complains about her situation, failing to see the grace of God in her life (expressed in part by the daughter-in-law who stands beside her). We wonder if the bitter one will ever become sweet again.

The word "bitter" leads us to an interesting parallel reference in one of **Job**'s speeches: "As God lives, who has taken away my right, and the Almighty, who has made my soul bitter…" (Job 27:2; see also 6:4). Job goes on to say that he will not sin with his lips but will maintain his integrity in the midst of his pain (27:3-5). He is certain that he has done nothing to be ashamed of. By contrast, Naomi is not able to insist on her own innocence. Like Job, she blames the Lord for her bitterness, but unlike him she cannot claim that she has not deserved it—although at the same time she does not actively admit that she has done anything wrong.

Sometimes when my wife is feeling frustrated (usually with our children), she will call and say, "Can I vent?" I allow her to, and it seems to help things. Naomi, too, is having a venting session; she repeats the word "Mara" or "bitter," adding, "The Almighty has dealt very bitterly with me" (Ruth **1:20b**). She attributes her pain to God: "I went away full, and the LORD has brought me back empty. Why call me Naomi, when the LORD has testified against me and the Almighty has brought calamity upon me?" (**v 21**). Strikingly, there is no acknowledgment of personal accountability—no mention of leaving Bethlehem for Moab, of staying in Moab, or of marrying her sons to Moabite women. She has shifted the blame entirely to Yahweh, using the title Shadday ("Almighty," an abbreviation for *El Shadday*), which denotes the cosmic ruler over all (see Job 5:17; Isaiah 13:6; Joel 1:15). She feels as though the Lord has held her to account in his courtroom ("testified against me"). Perhaps she uses this language because deep down she knows that he has a valid accusation against her. But, again, she does not admit this.

Naomi believes the Lord has made her life bitter. When she left, she was "full," but now he has made her "empty" (Ruth **1:21**). Of course, she was not full physically when she left—after all, there was a famine. But she was full with family and security, having a husband and two sons. She had a happy family when she left. But not anymore. She is empty. She has nothing—or at least that is what she thinks. She can only see her poverty, her lack of husband and sons, and her lack of security. She pits herself against God, even though it is part of God's character to care for widows (Exodus 22:21-23; see also Psalm 68:5; 146:9).

> Naomi may not be seeing things clearly, but she does see God in her situation.

While Naomi's venting session may be unpleasant to read, we should notice that she is no atheist! She does not blame "chance" nor an impersonal fate but God himself. She may not be seeing things clearly, and she definitely does not see things completely, but she at least sees God in her situation. However, her misconception lies in her failure to see God's compassion and his commitment to his people.

"She does indeed ascribe sovereignty to God, but this is a sovereignty without grace, an **omnipotent** power without compassion, a judicial will without mercy."

(Block, *Judges, Ruth*, page 647)

She returns to her name: "Why call me Naomi?" (Ruth **1:21b**). *Do not call me lovely or sweetie, for that is not my condition!* Can you imagine being one of the people of Bethlehem, looking at Naomi as she says this? What kind of response would you give? I would probably say nothing. It would be hard to know what to say.

For now, Naomi views God as the cosmic troublemaker, who has brought this "calamity" on her. There is no mention of Ruth and the pain she too has gone through. While we may admire Naomi's honesty, Ruth is the nobler example. Duguid rightly says of Naomi, "Her body may have made the journey home, but her spirit was far from restored" (*Esther & Ruth*, page 145).

The Barley Harvest

The narrator now offers his own comment. "So Naomi returned, and Ruth the Moabite her daughter-in-law with her, who returned from the country of Moab" (**v 22**). The return trip is complete. Naomi and her daughter-in-law have arrived in Bethlehem. Ruth is called for the first time "Ruth the Moabite"—a name which will be used repeatedly throughout the book (2:2, 21; 4:5, 10). This title reminds us of the ethnic tension and anticipates the drama to come.

Then we read a word of hope. The narrator gives us the season: "They came to Bethlehem at the beginning of barley harvest" (**1:22**). The physical famine at the beginning of the chapter also illustrated the spiritual famine in Naomi's life and the grief she experienced. Now there is a new beginning agriculturally. Will it be a new beginning in other ways for these women? Will Ruth find a husband? Will the family line extend? Will this harvest also bring about a harvest of grace in Naomi's life? Will her bitterness be replaced with joyful praise? Will this hopeless woman experience God's surprising grace? Those hearing the story for the first time will perk up with hope, pondering how things may turn out.

Questions for reflection

1. What does the word "bitter" make you think of?

2. When we feel the way Naomi did, how can we remind ourselves of God's grace?

3. What would you say to someone who speaks about God in the way Naomi did?

PART TWO

"Just one more episode." My wife and I have uttered those words on many occasions, after finishing one of our favorite shows (usually a British mystery). The reader feels that way after walking through Ruth 1; we want to know what happens next. But before we continue to chapter 2, we are first going to pause with some concluding reflections on chapter 1.

The focus throughout Ruth 1 has been on the grief and bitterness of Naomi. The first five verses explain her suffering, concluding with the words "The woman was left without her two sons and her husband." The following section displays the anguish she feels as she expresses her lack of hope (1:11-12) and her anger at the Lord (v 13). Even the astonishing commitment of Ruth does not make Naomi feel better, and when she reaches Bethlehem, she emphasizes again the bitterness she feels (**v 20-21**).

We are hoping that things will turn out better for Naomi—that the glimpses of God's providence that we have seen so far will develop into a greater restoration—and indeed in the next chapter we will see her situation improve. But Naomi herself could not simply read on to the next chapter. When you are filled with bitterness, it feels as though it will last forever.

So as we pause at the end of chapter 1, it is worth considering again how Naomi feels. We, too, sometimes experience this sense of utter emptiness. What should we do, and where should we turn, when calamity is brought upon us?

When God Seems Hidden

Several times in the first chapter of *Ruth*, Naomi acknowledges God and his power (v 8, 13, **21**); but she does not understand why he has done what he has done.

Of course, it is normal for God's people sometimes to wonder where God is, and what God is doing. Laments are understandable.

Naomi is not the only person who has questioned the purposes of God. The psalmists ask similar questions:

- "Why, O LORD, do you stand far away? Why do you hide yourself in times of trouble?" (Psalm 10:1)

- "How long, O LORD? Will you forget me forever? How long will you hide your face from me?" (13:1)

- "Awake! Why are you sleeping, O Lord? Rouse yourself! Do not reject us forever! Why do you hide your face? Why do you forget our affliction and oppression?" (44:23-24)

Sometimes God's hiddenness or the sense of God's absence is a result of sin, as we see in Psalm 51 (v 9, 11), but this is not always the case. At other times, God's hiddenness simply involves God's purposes being unclear. The obscurity of God's ways is expressed most clearly in Job 38: God challenges Job's complaints by listing all the things he does not understand about God and the world he has made. God does not always answer our questions. He never answered all of Job's.

Another way in which God may seem to be hidden in *Ruth* lies in the fact that he does not appear to be directly driving the action in the way that he does in books such as Exodus. We don't hear God speak at all. This is because, in certain books and passages of the Bible, God works "behind the scenes." We do not always read of miraculous events, of God's direct speech, or of God's direct intervention. In the book of Esther we do not read of God speaking or doing anything at all! Yet the hiddenness of God must not be mistaken for the absence of God.

In *Ruth*, God is active in the ordinariness of life. We see God's activity in two primary ways: the narrator's comments and the words and actions of the characters. The narrator mentions the Lord twice. Naomi heard that the Lord had visited the people with food (Ruth 1:6); and at the end of the story we will read that the Lord "gave her conception" (4:13). These are two remarkable bookends! God provides food, and then he provides a son. In between these two events, we should understand that God is providentially at work in the ordinariness of life, accomplishing his sovereign purposes, though we may perceive him to be hidden.

The characters in *Ruth*, too, highlight God's involvement in the ordinariness of life. We have seen how Naomi prays for the Lord's blessing on Orpah and Ruth (1:9). Then she directs her complaints to the Lord (v 13). She does not quite understand her perceived emptiness, but she keeps the Lord on our minds (**v 20-21**). In chapter 2, Naomi will be given hope when Boaz is mentioned and then offer a prayer for him:, "May he be blessed by the LORD" (2:20). Later the women of the town will say to her, "Blessed be the LORD, who has not left you this day without a **redeemer**" (4:14). God is at work in this widow's life, though here in chapter 1 she does not yet see this.

Ruth's conversion, too, shows us God's activity (1:16-18). It is a pivotal event in this whole storyline, and it is clearly a work of grace. Naomi's speeches in verses 8-13 show that there is no earthly reason for Ruth to put her trust in Yahweh; yet she does. As with every person who comes to faith, the conversion is God's work. Ruth was chosen by God before the foundation of the world (Ephesians 1:4).

When Boaz enters the story in Ruth 2, he too will keep the Lord before us. After Ruth enters his field, Boaz blesses his workers with the words, "The LORD be with you!" (Ruth 2:4), reminding us that God is present even in the ordinariness of everyday agricultural work. He also mentions Ruth's faith in the Lord and acknowledges the Lord's reward for faithfulness (v 11-12). In chapter 3, he says to Ruth, "May you be blessed by the LORD" (3:10) and places his commitment to act within the framework of his faith in God, saying, "As the LORD lives, I will redeem you" (v 13).

Much of *Ruth* looks very ordinary: we read about bread, family, death, daughters-in-law, widowhood, gossip, grief, bitterness, a baby, and other familiar things. But in truth *Ruth* magnifies God's providence. God is at work in this ordinary family. *Ruth* tells us not to dismiss or despise the ordinary but to look within it for God's extraordinary providence.

So, do not underestimate the value of joining a local church, and serving week by week without being noticed or praised. God is at work among his "ordinary saints." Do not forget that lives can be changed when you sit at the dinner table over a bowl of soup, when you chat with a neighbor on your morning walk, when you host a neighborhood cookout, when you volunteer to tutor at a local elementary school, and in countless other seemingly insignificant activities. Do not forget that you cannot always see what God is doing. We need to learn this. Many Christians tend to be drawn to the sensational, which is often hollow or shallow, and fail to miss God's work in the ho-hum of life, which is often glorious. While you may prefer the miraculous days of Exodus to the mundane days of *Ruth*, do not think for a moment that God is not at work in your ordinary life. John Piper says, "God is always doing 10,000 things in your life, and you may be aware of three of them" ("God Is Always Doing 10,000 Things in Life", www.desiringgod.org).

Looking Back with Joy

Like Naomi, we may want to call ourselves "Mara" at times. When we feel this way, we need to remember the Lord's grace. One wonderful way of doing this is to read the stories in the Old Testament. Remembering the ways God has worked in the past will help us to get better at being aware of the way God is working in the present.

When Naomi called herself "Mara," she would have been helped if she had paused to reflect on Israel's experience at Mara. That whole event should bring hope to despairing people. Not only did the Lord miraculously provide drinkable water, but he also took them to a place of natural rest and beauty: Elim (Exodus 15:27). The writer of Exodus notes the sight of seventy palm trees and springs of water. In the midst of the desert, the Lord took his people to a place of abundance and refreshment. He first provided a miracle at Mara and then provided through more ordinary means at Elim. In both cases the Lord transformed his people's experience.

But Naomi does not think of that story. Likewise, sadly, many Christians give little attention to the Old Testament. The few sermons they do hear from it usually focus on moral lessons drawn from Bible characters. They rarely hear an **expositional** series through Old Testament books which both highlights the selected text and shows how it relates to the overarching storyline of redemption. And some even go so far as to advocate that we "unhitch" ourselves from the Old Testament. This is essentially a new form of Marcionism, an ancient **heresy** that rejected the Old Testament (as well as much of the New).

But we must stay hitched to this section of Scripture. Stories such as that of the **exodus** remind us of what God is like and how he acts. Even more importantly, the Old Testament leads us toward, and helps us understand, the glorious story of our Messiah.

In his book *Preaching Christ from the Old Testament*, Sidney Greidanus offers six reasons why Christians should study the Old Testament (page 207):

1. The Old Testament is part of the Christian canon.

2. The Old Testament discloses the history of redemption leading to Christ.

3. The Old Testament proclaims truths not found in the New Testament.

4. The Old Testament helps us understand the New Testament.

5. The Old Testament prevents misunderstanding of the New Testament.

6. The Old Testament provides a fuller understanding of Christ.

Each of these points is important, but numbers 2, 4, and 6 are especially important when you consider the fact that Ruth appears in the genealogy of Jesus in Matthew 1:5. The book of *Ruth* highlights the reality that the Old Testament shows us the story of the Messiah. We have the privilege of zooming in on one person's life in *Ruth*. We get to read of her origins, her grief, her remarkable conversion, her relationship with Naomi, and (soon) her marriage to Boaz, leading to the birth of a son. But *Ruth* closes with a genealogy that links this story to King David. When we read Matthew 1:5, we see a longer version of the same genealogy; then we marvel at the history of redemption, which leads at last to Christ. *Ruth* helps us understand this genealogy better and thus have a greater appreciation for the arrival of Jesus Christ. The **incarnation** is seen to be more marvelous if you stay hitched to the Old Testament.

While Naomi could have looked back on the exodus events to remind herself of God's compassion and commitment, we can now look back on an even greater story: Jesus' incarnation, crucifixion, resurrection, and ascension. At the crucifixion, Jesus quoted Psalm 22, which is perhaps the most famous lament in the Psalms: "My God, my God, why have you forsaken me?" (Psalm 22:1a). The Father was silent as Jesus cried out on the cross. But at the cross we see again that God is working out his saving purposes through the actions of others, though it might seem as though he is hidden (see Acts 2:23). If you ever have a Naomi experience—believing God is absent or incomprehensible—then look to the cross. Turn your eyes to Jesus, the One who was abandoned and crucified that we may be reconciled to God forever, and hold on to the promise that he will never leave us nor forsake us (Hebrews 13:5).

> If you ever believe God is absent or incomprehensible, look to the cross and hold on to the promise that he will never leave us.

One of the reasons why in my church we recite either the **Apostles' creed**, the **Nicene creed**, or various **creeds** from the Bible (such as Philippians 2:5-11) every week is to remind ourselves of these glorious truths, and of the truths of what Jesus will do on his return. The ultimate answer to our bitterness is not a change of circumstances. It is found in the Lord. How on earth could Paul have urged the Philippians to "rejoice" (Philippians 3:1; 4:4) while he sat chained in prison, if he had not known that joy is obtained "in the Lord," regardless of circumstances—through resting in him and finding our satisfaction in him?

The real empty one was Christ. He emptied himself (Philippians 2:5-11), leaving heaven for earth, in order that we may receive full forgiveness and eternal life. He took the judgment against us on himself, and by faith in him we receive his righteousness. Believers now have a totally new identity and status as sons and daughters of the King. We must not forget the grace of God in the gospel! Grace does not just get us into heaven later; it also gets heaven into us now. We will die in gospel hope, but with gospel hope we can also live.

Yet we will not experience the power of this living hope if we fail to remember. How quickly God's people forgot what God had done for them; how quickly we, too, can forget! This is why Paul tells a discouraged Timothy, "Remember Jesus Christ, risen from the dead, the offspring of David" (2 Timothy 2:8).

In our bitterness, we must remember. This is why we sing songs of God's grace, listen to sermons about God's grace, and speak his gospel to one another as a community of faith. This is also why we take the **Lord's Supper** regularly in our local churches. Jesus gave us this sacred ordinance to help us never to forget what he has done for us. It is when we ponder deeply the sacrifice of Christ that thankfulness, in place of bitterness, fills our hearts.

It is when we think deeply about what God has done for us that we realize that we are not alone in this world. Immanuel, "God with us," has come for us and has poured out his Holy Spirit upon us. Believers in Christ have the indwelling presence of the Comforter, even when our lives are filled with hardship and grief. We have a greater way of dealing with bitterness than self-help therapy or the changing of our external circumstances: we have the gospel.

Looking Forward with Hope

In our trials, we are able not only to look back at what God has done for us in Christ but also to look ahead to the future. Think how things would have looked to Naomi if she had known the future of her family. Not only would the Messiah come from this particular line; this Messiah—the one called "The Lion of the tribe of Judah, the Root of David" (Revelation 5:5)—will come again in glory. At his first coming, he was a baby born in Bethlehem. At his second, he will be the conquering King of kings.

We know this because we know far more about the future than Naomi and Ruth knew. The purpose of eschatology (literally "the study of last things") is not to incite wild fanaticism but to inspire present faithfulness during suffering. The scholar G.K. Beale says of the book of Revelation:

"The main point of the whole book is that faithful endurance and obedience to the end will result in eternal blessing and reward, with the ultimate result of glorifying God and Christ."

(*The Book of Revelation*, page 1157)

Revelation gives us a glorious vision of heaven that motivates us to be faithful to the end. While there are many aspects to this final book of the Bible, the overall message is clear: Jesus is coming; therefore, be faithful! When you are struggling with grief and pain like Naomi, remember that Jesus wins, and all who are in him—"those who are written in the **Lamb**'s book of life"—win with him (Revelation 21:27).

We must remember this ending during those times when the process of winning may feel like losing. Sometimes I watch my favorite teams play games on ESPN Classic. This channel regularly shows old games. If you are watching your team play a game in which they are losing badly, but you know that they come from behind to win, you watch that game very differently than the way you watched it live! You are stressed when you do not know the outcome, but when you do know it, you can relax. In a very real sense, the Christian life is one in which we know the outcome. We do not know everything about the future, to be sure. But we do know that Jesus wins, and that all who are in him win with him. We do know that Jesus will wipe the tears from our eyes, and there will be no more dying, no more grief, and no more pain. It is this that allows us to "rejoice in hope, be patient in tribulation, [and] be constant in prayer" (Romans 12:12).

Questions for reflection

1. How should we respond when God seems hidden?

2. If someone asked you about how God has worked in the past, what would you say? Would you talk about the Old Testament? The work of Jesus? Your own experiences?

3. How can you help yourself to look forward with hope this week?

4. THE FIELD

The first chapter of *Ruth* dealt primarily with three women, but now the narrative widens to include the whole community. We are introduced to a "worthy man," Boaz, in the first verse (**2:1**). It is as if the author is saying, *Keep your eye on this guy!*

As we read Ruth 2, we need to keep in mind the darkness of the days of the judges, so that we will be even more impressed by Boaz's integrity, his protection of the vulnerable, and his compassion for the poor. Boaz was different than many of the men of his day. We, too, need a new generation of men like him. These words of the psalmist could be said of Boaz:

> "Blessed is the man who fears the LORD, who greatly delights in his commandments! His offspring will be mighty in the land; the generation of the upright will be blessed … It is well with the man who deals generously and lends; who conducts his affairs with justice … He has distributed freely; he has given to the poor; his righteousness endures forever; his **horn** is exalted in honor." (Psalm 112:1-2; 5, 9)

These are some key marks of godliness. This description certainly reflects the character of Boaz.

But there is more to Boaz than a model of justice; he is also a picture of Christ. So as we look at Boaz, we also want to look through Boaz, so that we may see our Savior. Boaz's grace points to Jesus' grace—the grace that has bought our salvation, and the grace that strengthens and empowers us to love this broken world. Jesus, in his kindness, has sought the outcast, has given us refuge, has fed us at his table, and has become our Redeemer. Now, in Christ, we have a new status and are empowered to live a righteous life to God's glory.

Like Ruth 1, chapter 2 involves a series of conversations. There are five dialogues: Ruth tells Naomi of her plan to go out to the fields (Ruth **2:2-3**); Boaz greets his reapers and learns about Ruth (**v 4-7**); Boaz offers Ruth protection (v 8-15); Boaz tells the reapers to help her (v 15b-16); and Ruth tells Naomi all that has happened (v 19-22). In terms of subject matter, three themes stand out all the way through: faith, favor, and hope. In this chapter, we will discuss the first three of these conversations, and seek to understand the favor Boaz shows and the faith of both him and Ruth. In the following chapter we will move to the last two dialogues, seeing how hope rises for Ruth and Naomi, and how Boaz's favor points to the greater favor of God.

For behind it all is the hero of the story: the Lord. He is accomplishing his purposes. His providence is revealed beautifully in chapter 2. The Lord provides Boaz as the answer to Naomi's prayer, and the solution to the crisis of the family line.

A Worthy Man

We read, first of all, that Boaz was a relative of Naomi's husband. He was "of the clan of Elimelech" (**v 1**). This phrase is significant. Later in the chapter, Naomi tells Ruth that Boaz "is one of our redeemers" (v 20; see also 3:9, 12). Boaz is a legal relative of Elimelech, which proves to be crucial in the narrative, due to Israelite laws and customs.

The meaning of Boaz's name is debated, though most suggestions point to the idea of "strength." No one else in the Hebrew Bible bears this name. Many claim it carries the idea of "strong spirit," or "in him [Yahweh] is strength" (Hubbard, *The Book of Ruth*, page 134; Dale Ralph Davis, *1 Kings*, page 73). In 1 Kings we read of Hiram making some items for the temple, including a pair of massive pillars (1 Kings 7:13-22; 2 Chronicles 3, especially v 17). One pillar was called "Jachin" ("He will establish") and the other "Boaz" ("In him is strength"). I think these names signified a message. These pillars conveyed the firmness of

God's promise to establish David's throne (see 2 Samuel 7:12-16) and God's mighty strength to accomplish it. David's royal Psalm 21 begins and ends with this word "Boaz" ("strength" in English): "O LORD, in your strength the king rejoices … Be exalted, O LORD, in your strength!" (Psalm 21:1, 13). When the people saw this pillar, they may have indeed thought of Psalm 21. Therefore, standing in front of the temple proper were these two pillars, "He will establish" and "In him is strength"— the promise of God and the power of God exalted. The story of Ruth does show God's power to make his promises come to pass, and he uses Boaz as part of this plan. Further, the story of Ruth and Boaz clearly shows Boaz to be a man of godly strength.

Not only is Boaz a relative, but he is also a "worthy man" (Ruth **2:1**). This phrase is interpreted in a variety of ways. The meaning usually carries the idea of "war hero." The picture of a mighty warrior, though, is probably not the best explanation here. The phrase can also mean "capable person" and "wealthy man." The story clearly shows Boaz to be a man of wealth and influence, having standing in the community (4:1-3, 9, 11). He does not fight battles (like **Gideon**, of whom the same Hebrew phrase is used in Judges 6:12), but he does own property and have servants. But there must be more than just wealth and influence in view; the same word is used to describe Ruth (Ruth 3:11), who was poor. Boaz is not just a wealthy man; he is also a man with integrity and godliness. In short, he is a man of both moral worth and material wealth.

So **2:1** introduces us to some key features of Boaz. Both his selfless character and his wealth will prove vital as the story unfolds. Further, he is a relative of Naomi and therefore a possible "redeemer," which will be important—the narrator and the characters repeat this word for us (v 20; 3:9, 12-13).

Ruth's Faith

In **2:2**, "Ruth the Moabite" enters the story again. While we are keeping our eye on Boaz, it would be a mistake not to keep a close watch on Ruth as well. Perhaps you can identify with her. She is a new believer. She does not have any money. She has left her family behind. She does not come from the best of families. She is single and a widow. But her faith shines in this chapter. As we look at her, we will see that God did something for Ruth, in Ruth, and eventually through Ruth. He provided Boaz for her, he worked humility and faith in her, and he brought the eventual Messiah through her.

By calling Ruth "the Moabite," the author reminds us of the ethnic tension in the story, which highlights the gutsy faith of Ruth. She is a courageous, compassionate, humble, loyal, and hardworking immigrant. Circumstances are against her. Five times she is called "the Moabite" (1:22; **2:2**, 21; 4:5, 10). She is not only an outsider but also a widow in the **patriarchal** society of Israel. But Ruth's faith, like all true faith, leads her to act. She turns to Naomi and says, "Let me go to the field and glean among the ears of grain after him in whose sight I shall find favor" (**2:2**). This is the attitude of real faith. She is dependent on the goodwill of a landowner, and ultimately on the Lord.

Gleaning consisted of gathering dropped grain or grain left standing. The harvesters were to leave the edges of the field for the poor and not retrieve dropped crops. We read of these instructions:

"When you reap your harvest in your field and forget a sheaf in the field, you shall not go back to get it. It shall be for the **sojourner**, the fatherless, and the widow, that the LORD your God may bless you in all the work of your hands. When you beat your olive trees, you shall not go over them again. It shall be for the sojourner, the fatherless, and the widow. When you gather the grapes of your vineyard, you shall not strip it afterward. It shall be for the sojourner, the fatherless, and the widow. You shall remember that you were a slave in the land of Egypt; therefore I command you to do this." (Deuteronomy 24:19-22)

"When you reap the harvest of your land, you shall not reap your field right up to its edge, neither shall you gather the gleanings after your harvest. And you shall not strip your vineyard bare, neither shall you gather the fallen grapes of your vineyard. You shall leave them for the poor and for the sojourner: I am the LORD your God." (Leviticus 19:9-10)

The law made provision for the poor, the widow, and the sojourner, and so Ruth was qualified to "glean" in the fields. The system also required effort and work on the part of the poor. They were not going to improve their status by picking up scraps, but they could survive. It is similar to recycling aluminum cans today. Perhaps you have seen those struggling to make ends meet doing this. Some work very hard just to eke out an existence. Now imagine a poor immigrant picking up cans who meets and ends up marrying a wealthy business-owner in the community! That would be a great movie.

We are not told how much of this law Ruth knew. The Israelites, though, should have been familiar with this provision for the vulnerable, and with God's concern for the orphan, widow, and stranger (Exodus 22:21-22; Psalm 146:9). However, some landowners still were not friendly to the idea of the poor gleaning in their fields (Deuteronomy 27:19; Isaiah 1:17). Remember that we are in the dark times of the judges; everyone was doing what was right in their own eyes, and we should not assume that the laws about gleaning were widely put into practice.

Ruth certainly does not go to the fields with a sense of entitlement but with humility. She plans to approach a landowner, someone in a superior position, hoping that he will be gracious to her. She recognizes her need for favor. The word "favor" appears three times in our passage. Here in Ruth **2:2**, Ruth seeks favor. In verse 10, she finds favor; and in verse 13, she recognizes that Boaz will continue to show her favor. Ruth could have sung this hymn:

Praise him for his grace and favor
To our fathers in distress;
Praise him still the same as ever,
Slow to chide, and swift to bless.
Praise him, praise him, alleluia!
Glorious in his faithfulness. (Henry Lyte)

Ruth's meeting with Boaz is a meeting between humility and grace, and the two go together. The biblical writers emphasize the centrality of humility in the life of the believer. Ruth's life illustrates the proverb "Toward the scorners he is scornful, but to the humble he gives favor" (Proverbs 3:34); and the words of James: "God opposes the proud but gives grace to the humble" (James 4:6; see also 1 Peter 5:5). God is attracted to humility. He gives it his attention. Arrogance and entitlement receive his opposition. Instead we should follow Ruth's example of humility, being desperate for God's grace.

> Ruth's meeting with Boaz is a meeting between humility and grace, and the two go together.

Gleaning was hard work, embarrassing, and not always safe, especially for a foreigner. Think of a single woman today going into a male-dominated work context. In many places and countries, this would be a disaster in the making. This was all the more the case in Ruth's times. She was vulnerable. She had no family to protect her. Yet she stepped out in faith, hoping to meet a generous landowner.

Ruth **2:3** shows how Ruth found such a landowner. After Naomi encouraged her to enter the fields (Ruth **2:2**), "she set out and went and gleaned in the field after the reapers, and she happened to come to the part of the field belonging to Boaz, who was of the clan of Elimelech" (**v 3**). Don't miss this: she "happened" to enter Boaz's field. Literally the Hebrew reads, "and her chance chanced upon the allotted portion of the field of Boaz." As we might say, "As luck would have it." Of course, the narrator does not believe in chance but providence. The Lord controls even the roll of the dice (Proverbs 16:9, 33). The whole Bible views the world as coming under the fatherly sovereignty of God. Jesus says that not a sparrow drops without the Father's knowledge (Matthew 10:29).

So why does the writer of *Ruth* use this phrase? Block argues that this is one of the most important phrases in the book.

"By excessively attributing Ruth's good fortune to chance, he forces the reader to sit up and take notice, to ask questions concerning the significance of everything that is transpiring ... In reality he is screaming, 'See the hand of God at work here!' The same hand that had sent the famine ([Ruth] 1:1) and later provided food (1:6) is the hand that had brought Naomi and Ruth to Bethlehem precisely at the beginning of the harvest (1:22) and has now guided Ruth to that portion of the field belonging specifically to Boaz." (*Judges, Ruth*, pages 653-654)

Notice that the phrase "of the clan of Elimelech" is used again in **2:3**. Ruth does not yet realize it, but she has entered the fields of a relative: one of the few men who is able to give her and Naomi the help they need.

God's quiet hand is always at work. He is not just at work in the miraculous, when water flows from a rock. He is also at work as a desperate Moabite widow finds her way to the field of a generous redeemer named Boaz.

This is Ruth's faith. Her faith acted (**v 2a**). Her faith meant she knew she had desperate need for grace (**v 2b**). And her faith was laced with humility. As Boaz would express it later, Ruth's life of faith began when she took refuge under the wings of the Lord (v 12). Her profession of faith in chapter 1 thus proves genuine in chapter 2.

Boaz's Faith

The narrator tells us that Boaz's timing was perfect, and if you catch his emphasis of divine providence, you realize that this is because God's timing is perfect. There is a note of wonder with the word "Behold," preparing us to hear that "Boaz came from Bethlehem" (**v 4**). "Mr. Right" appeared at just the right time.

We are given a brief glimpse of Boaz's character by the way he greets his workers: "The LORD be with you!" And they answer, "The LORD bless you." Here is our first impression of Boaz—he greets his workers in the name of Yahweh. This does not seem to be empty religious talk. The narrator is frugal with his words: he leaves out many things, and so what he does include is always significant, including this little greeting. Boaz repeats the great covenant promise of God, "I will be with you," which is woven throughout the Bible (for example, Deuteronomy 31:9; Joshua 1:5; Isaiah 43:2) and finally seen in Jesus, Immanuel, "God with us" (Matthew 1:23), who promises to be with us until the end of the age (Matthew 28:18-20; Revelation 21:3). Boaz is saying, *Remember the presence and blessing of God in this field!* The workers respond to him with a similar greeting. We are left to anticipate great things from this Boaz.

Boaz's religion is not a once-a-week kind of thing. His spiritual life is not just about a "morning **quiet time**" either. He seems to have Yahweh on his mind even in the midst of the fields, in the ordinary routine of life. Imagine an office in which the boss greets all the people in the cubicles in this way! Wouldn't that be wonderful?!

Like Boaz, we should do our work with the Lord's glory and grace on our minds. We should use our words to build up and bless others at work. We must show our faith not just during corporate worship but also by how we approach our work during the week.

Questions for reflection

1. Reflect on how God provides for the vulnerable (pages 64-65). What would be the equivalent of leaving grain in the fields today?

2. What do you most admire about Ruth in this passage? How could you imitate her?

3. What do you most admire about Boaz? How could you imitate him?

PART TWO

A Worthy Woman

With Boaz introduced to us, next we see how he becomes aware of Ruth's presence in his fields. He asks his foreman about this strange woman: "Whose young woman is this?" (Ruth **2:5**). Notice that he does not approach Ruth directly, nor does he ask the foreman her name. He asks the foreman to whom this "young" woman belongs. (Ruth is apparently younger than Boaz.) He wants to know something of her origins. He does not recognize her as the daughter-in-law of Naomi. In **verses 11-12** it becomes clear that he has heard all about Ruth and what she has done for her mother-in-law, but here he does not make the connection between the woman he has heard about and the woman he sees in his field. All he notices at this point is that she is out of place and by herself. It seems that he is concerned for her even before he knows about her situation and her character.

The foreman gives Boaz an explanation of who Ruth is. He notes Ruth's ethnicity, her connection to Naomi, and her desire to glean in the field (**v 6-7**). He also emphasizes her impressive work ethic (**v 7**): she has had only a short rest all day. Here is another mark of Ruth's faith and humility: hard work. Faith in Yahweh does not mean being lazy and waiting around for him to act. Ruth tries to make the very best of her situation that she can, trusting God to be good to her as she does so. She exemplifies the diligence of the virtuous woman of Proverbs 31.

The foreman's report speaks highly of Ruth's character. The scene is now set for Boaz and Ruth's first conversation. How will this "worthy," God-fearing man treat this vulnerable, faithful, hard-working woman?

Boaz Favors Ruth

On hearing the foreman's words, Boaz decides to show favor to Ruth. This is expressed in a remarkable commitment to give protection and provision to her. After tenderly addressing Ruth as "my daughter" (Ruth **2:8**), Boaz authorizes her freedom to glean in his field, along with his own workers. Here is an example of a man obeying God's word in a day in which "everyone did what was right in his own eyes" (Judges 21:25).

Boaz does not only tell Ruth that she may glean in his field but actually insists that she stay there, telling her to "keep close to my young women" and "go after" them (Ruth **2:8-9**). He is determined to provide for her. He also shows her where to find water for refreshment. He is like the boss showing his new employee where everything is located in the building, including the break room. His word about drawing water is striking. Normally foreigners would draw water for Israelites, and women would draw it for men (Genesis 24:10-20). But she is given the freedom to drink from water already drawn by the Israelites.

Boaz not only provides work and water for Ruth but also protection. This is displayed by how he orders the men not to touch or harass Ruth. She is to be welcomed and protected, and not violated in any way. Block says:

> "Contemporary readers will be struck by how modern this comment sounds. Boaz is hereby instituting the first anti-sexual-harassment policy in the workplace recorded in the Bible."
>
> (*Judges, Ruth*, page 660)

We are not told of Boaz's motivations at this point, but only of his kindness and concern for Ruth's wellbeing. But these words are overwhelming to Ruth. She has been through so much hardship. Now she hears these gracious words from Boaz. In response, she falls on her face, bowing to the ground—a sign of deep gratitude. She asks, "Why have I found favor in your eyes, that you should take notice of me, since I am a foreigner?" (Ruth **2:10**). She cannot believe that such grace has been shown to an outsider like her. Boaz is the very sort of person Ruth hoped to find when she went out to glean: someone "in whose sight I shall find favor" (v 2). But the fact that she is so overwhelmed suggests that she did not expect to find such provision and protection as this. She has truly stepped out in faith, and her faith has been rewarded.

When humility and grace meet, worship begins. We have received God's grace in an even greater way than Ruth, as recipients of Jesus' saving grace (Ephesians 2:1-22). We should be even more overcome with gratitude when we consider how the Savior has met our greatest need. We should fall on our knees often, asking, "Why have I found favor in your eyes, that you should take notice of me?"

Boaz's Motives

In addition to material provision, Boaz goes on to show favor to Ruth in another way. He blesses her with his words (Ruth **2:11-14**). You can imagine what the affirmation of a godly, influential leader must have sounded like to her. His encouragement surely lifted her spirits and gave her a sense of dignity.

Boaz first speaks of Ruth's reputation. He had heard about Ruth's experience: how she had cared for Naomi, how she lost her husband, and how she had left her native land to join a new people (**v 11**). Word had spread about Ruth, and Boaz was impressed; so he express-es his admiration to her. Professor Hubbard adds that Boaz's words recall Abraham and Sarah's migration in Genesis 12:1-5:

"Now the LORD said to Abram, 'Go from your country and your kindred and your father's house to the land that I will show you. And I will make of you a great nation, and I will bless you and make your name great, so that you will be a blessing. I will bless those who bless you, and him who dishonors you I will curse, and in you all the families of the earth shall be blessed.'

"So Abram went, as the Lord had told him, and Lot went with him. Abram was seventy-five years old when he departed from Haran. And Abram took Sarai his wife, and Lot his brother's son, and all their possessions that they had gathered, and the people that they had acquired in Haran, and they set out to go to the land of Canaan."

Maybe God viewed Ruth in a similar light. Ruth would indeed emerge as another great matriarch in Israel like Sarah (see Hubbard, *The Book of Ruth*, page 165).

Boaz continues to encourage Ruth by praying that God will reward her faith. He says, "The LORD repay you for what you have done, and a full reward be given you by the LORD, the God of Israel, under whose wings you have come to take refuge!" (Ruth **2:12**). He is not demanding reward from the Lord but humbly offering his desire to him. Boaz believes that Ruth's actions deserve more than just his own recognition. He longs for the Lord to reward her in full. The language here also has an echo of Jacob's wage disputes with his father-in-law, Laban (see Genesis 29:15; 31:7, 41). If that is intended, then Boaz is again relating Ruth's life and faith to those of the **patriarchs**.

Boaz believes that what Ruth has done is a result of her faith in God. It is the Lord whom she has pleased by her actions. Similarly, the writer of Hebrews says that without faith it is impossible to please God, and that God is a rewarder of those who seek him in faith (Hebrews 11:6). The fact that God rewards faith is stated throughout Scripture (for example, Jeremiah 25:14; Psalm 28:4; Job 34:11; Proverbs 13:21; 19:17; 24:12, 25:22; Romans 2:6-9; 2 Corinthians 5:10). While faith-fueled actions may go unnoticed by other people, they do not go unnoticed by the Lord. We should not live for the approval and praise of others but for the glory of God, who knows all, sees all, and in the end rewards all who live by faith.

The Lord is not only a rewarder; he is also a refuge. Boaz commends Ruth for abandoning the Moabite gods and taking "refuge" under the "wings" of the God of Israel (Ruth **2:12**). This image of finding refuge under the Lord's wings carries the idea of God's protection and his nurturing care for his people—it is also used in this way in Deuteronomy 32:11-12. Likewise, in Exodus 19:4 the whole exodus deliverance is likened to the actions of an eagle: "You yourselves have seen what I did to the Egyptians, and how I bore you on eagles' wings and brought you to myself." Like Israel's ancestors, Ruth had entrusted herself to the power and grace of the Lord. Later in the Bible, this image is found again, as the psalmists express trust in the Lord for helping them in times of trouble (see Psalm 17:8; 36:7; 91:1-4; also 2:11; 118:8-9). In the New Testament a similar image is used by Jesus when he weeps over Jerusalem, saying that he longs to gather them as "a hen gathers her brood under her wings" (Matthew 23:37). How sad that people reject Christ's salvation and his rest. We should thank God for his rescue and protection, and tell the world where to go to find this eternal grace. Only in the Lord can we find salvation, rest, protection, and nurture.

In response to Boaz's kindness, Ruth expresses her gratitude, saying, "I have found favor in your eyes, my lord, for you have comforted me and spoken kindly to your servant, though I am not one of your servants" (Ruth **2:13**). Ruth expresses relief, humility, and a deep sense of thankfulness. She recognizes that she is not even one of Boaz's "servants," and yet he has blessed her in word and deed. Her race and her class did not prevent Boaz from showing her compassion. Ruth had had no idea what the day would bring, but by God's grace she found herself in a field of favor.

Looking at Boaz: Mercy and Justice

We find many personal applications for our lives in this section. Boaz and Ruth have given us a template for faith. Ruth does not wait around complaining of her difficulties but works hard to improve her situation, even while hoping that God will provide for her. She humbly recognizes her need for favor and is full of gratitude when it comes. Meanwhile, Boaz shows us what faith is like in the everyday. He is not in crisis, nor does he see miracles happen, but he does know that God is with him in his ordinary working life. He knows the character of God and seeks to serve him by pursuing a life of mercy and justice, noticing Ruth's vulnerability and going beyond what is necessary to provide for and protect her. We, too, can and should have faith that looks like that of Ruth and Boaz.

It is worth lingering on this point about mercy and justice. The prophet Micah summarized the Israelite **social ethic** in this way:

"He has told you, O man, what is good;
and what does the LORD require of you
but to do justice, and to love kindness,
and to walk humbly with your God?" (Micah 6:8).

Here in Ruth 2, Boaz gives us an example of Micah 6:8 in at least five ways.

First, Boaz provides for the hungry. He does justice by following the Lord's word regarding the widow, the stranger, and the poor, allowing Ruth gleaning rights. Many landowners were not friendly to this law. And it is easy to imagine how some may have justified to themselves their lack of provision for the poor, as they recovered from a ten-year famine! Yet Boaz obeyed the word to "do justice."

Second, Boaz not only provides for Ruth, but he also protects her. He serves as Ruth's justice advocate, charging the men not to harm her. Strangers and widows could easily be mistreated and abused—just as they still are around the world today—but Boaz offers her protection. Boaz thus reflects Proverbs 31:8-9, which tells us that "judg[ing] righteously" means "defend[ing] the rights of the poor and needy." He uses his influence for those who have no influence.

Third, Boaz uses his words to bless Ruth, showing her personal dignity and respect. He goes beyond the requirements of the law—he showers this desperate foreigner with grace. He offers Ruth refreshment (Ruth **2:9**); he honors her faith (**v 11**); he prays for her (**v 12**); and he speaks kindly to her (**v 13**). In the following verses, he even invites her to his table for food and fellowship (v 14). Finally, he urges the men to allow her to glean more than she ever imagined (v 15-16). This is more than justice: Boaz shows that he "love[s] kindness."

Fourth, Boaz shows kindness and grace not only to Ruth but also to his workers. Employers have much to learn from Boaz. His greeting to his workers in the field and their response indicate that his workers respect him. Boaz displays a good understanding of the need to "bring faith to work." This integration of the "sacred" and "secular" is badly needed today. Boaz does his work for the Lord, recognizing the Lord's grace in helping him to do it (see Colossians 3:17; 3:23 – 4:1).

Finally, Boaz walks humbly with the Lord. This is evidenced in many ways. His consideration of Ruth, his way of addressing his workers, his acknowledgement of the Lord's sovereignty, and, as we shall see, his willingness to eat with his workers, are expressions of a humble walk before the Lord. No wonder he and Ruth make such a good match! Humility is displayed in them both.

> May the Lord raise up a new generation of men like Boaz, who protect and provide for, and do not prey on, others.

One final word is needed about the way Boaz exemplifies Micah 6:8. He is a man who shows mercy and justice. As a result of sin having entered the world, men face the temptation to be either passive or abusive (or both, in different parts of their lives). While injustice is not just a male problem, it does exist in large measure due to men either causing it (being abusive) or failing to do it (being passive). When I attend orphan-care events and justice conferences, it always strikes me that the number of women usually exceeds the number of men present. I am very happy to see the women there; but fighting for justice, defending the powerless, providing for the poor, taking up for the oppressed, and giving a voice to the voiceless are not activities reserved for women only—because the command to love your neighbor as yourself is not reserved for women only!

May the Lord raise up a new generation of men like Boaz, who protect and provide for women, and do not prey on them. May the Lord give us a generation of men who display kindness and grace to all. May we pray for those men, and if we are men, strive to be them.

Thankfully, we are not left to struggle alone as we try to follow the examples of Ruth and Boaz and their extraordinary, ordinary faith. We may live this kind of life by the power of the greater Boaz, our Redeemer, Jesus Christ. In this chapter we have looked at Boaz; in the next we shall look through Boaz to the Savior, who makes this kind of life possible.

Questions for reflection

1. Why does the image of taking refuge under the wings of the Lord express what Ruth experienced? How could you describe your own faith journey in a way that emphasizes God's grace?

2. Which of the ways in which Boaz showed mercy and justice is the greatest challenge to you? How could you live out Micah 6:8?

3. How could Ruth 2:1-19 inform your prayers this week?

5. THE MEAL

The first half of Ruth 2 showed us the character of Boaz, a man of both moral worth and material wealth. He is a man who does mercy and justice for Ruth, the widow and foreigner, and a man who leads his workers admirably. The latter half of the chapter shows us these same character traits, but here, crucially, we also learn that Boaz is a "redeemer" (Ruth **2:20**). We will take a close look at this section in three parts:

1. Boaz's hospitality and generosity

2. Naomi's recognition of this kindness

3. Ruth and Naomi's hope

Following that, we will think more deeply about the concept of redemption and the role of our own Redeemer.

Boaz's Hospitality

Boaz's favor extends to the dinner table (**v 14**). In modern terms, we may want to think of this as Boaz and Ruth's first date! But this is not a nice romantic meal over some roasted grain—it is more like a lunch break at work. Even so, Boaz's hospitality is gracious and exemplary.

The narrator describes Boaz's welcome and provision: "And at mealtime Boaz said to her, 'Come here and eat some bread and dip your morsel in the wine.' So she sat beside the reapers, and he passed to her roasted grain." We do not know if Ruth even brought anything to eat. But Boaz meets her need and more. The writer says, "She was satisfied, and she had some left over." Leftovers! With whom is she going to share these? Naomi, of course (**v 18**)!

We learn a lot about Boaz from this touching scene. First, there is his style of leadership. Even though he is a wealthy boss, he still eats with his workers. This fact is an example of his noble character and his commendable leadership. He does not isolate himself from his workers. He associates with them—as Paul instructs Christians to do in Romans 12:16b.

Second, he not only eats alongside the workers, but he also acts as the host of the meal. He urges Ruth to eat of what has been provided and instructs her as to how to eat it ("Eat some bread and dip your morsel into the wine"). He also serves her the roasted grain personally (Ruth **2:14**). This says something about his attitude. He does not sit down with his workers but then give everyone the silent treatment or speak only to the most senior. He serves. He leads with grace. His attitude is one of humility and warmth—important traits of leaders.

Third, he provides more than enough. He is not a stingy leader. The scene is a picture of abundance, similar to what Mark says about Jesus' feeding of the 5,000: "And they all ate and were satisfied. And they took up twelve baskets full of broken pieces and of the fish" (Mark 6:42-43).

Fourth, Boaz not only grants Ruth the freedom to glean, but he welcomes her into his group of workers. He gives her a seat next to the reapers, which provides a sense of honor and dignity.

In all this, Boaz goes well beyond the requirements of the law, lavishing his grace upon Ruth. Block comments, "Boaz took an ordinary event and transformed it into a magnanimous occasion for compassion, generosity, and acceptance" (*The King Is Coming*, page 137). He exemplifies *hesed*—the same loving kindness that God shows to his people.

It is hard for many of us to adequately appreciate having enough food to satisfy our needs, since we have grown accustomed to eating three meals per day and keeping the refrigerator and kitchen cabinets stocked. But to a poor, desperate widow, this meal would have been absolutely wonderful. For once, Ruth did not have to worry about having enough food to eat. We should pause, thank God for our daily bread, and ask him to use us to bless those who are in need. Like Boaz, we must look to bless them not only materially but also relationally. We should serve the poor and the vulnerable with an attitude of warmth through the practice of hospitality. The poor need a sense of dignity, and they need friends, not just stuff.

After the meal, Ruth prepares to continue gleaning. Her activity initiates Boaz's instruction to his young men: "Let her glean even among the sheaves, and do not reproach her. And also pull out some from the bundles for her and leave it for her to glean, and do not rebuke her" (Ruth **2:15-16**). Again, Boaz goes beyond the letter of the law. He charges the workers not to insult or mistreat Ruth. He also gives Ruth the special privilege of gleaning "among the sheaves" (**v 15**; that is from "the grain among the bundles," CSB). Normally gleaning meant picking up grain that had been discarded or left behind accidentally by the harvesters, but here Ruth is invited to take the pick of the crop—the grain that has already been harvested. She will not have to work so hard to find dropped bits of grain. Boaz even tells the workers to pull some of the stalks from the bundles and leave them for Ruth to gather (**v 16**). He wants to make Ruth's job easier for her and more beneficial to her.

As a result, Ruth gathers an abundance: a whole "ephah of barley" (**v 17**). She brings home some thirty pounds (13.6kg) of food! That would be several weeks' worth of food. Ruth apparently hauls this back to Naomi's place all by herself. This Moabite can carry some grain!

Recognizing Kindness

Ruth had left Naomi to go and search for favor. She found it in Boaz. Now she returns to Naomi with leftovers and a load of barley (**v 18**). A conversation about her day and about Boaz ensues.

Before looking at that conversation, we should stop and consider Ruth's ongoing kindness to her mother-in-law. She is still with her and still serving her. Ruth shows the same kindness to Naomi that Boaz has shown to her. I find Ruth's example challenging. Do you find it hard to love bitter people? Is it challenging to serve difficult people? If so, then allow Ruth to instruct and inspire you! Love the "Naomis" in your life in the way that Christ has shown love to you, realizing that the proper response to his grace and patience toward you is to show grace and patience to others.

Naomi is, understandably, excited. She asks two questions and then, without waiting for a response, bursts out with a blessing: "Where did you glean today? And where have you worked? Blessed be the man who took notice of you" (**v 19**). Naomi's tone has changed dramatically in light of this evidence of grace.

Ruth replies to Naomi, explaining that Boaz was the benefactor. Naomi responds with two statements. Her first response repeats her blessing: "May he be blessed by the LORD, whose kindness has not forsaken the living or the dead!" (**v 20a**). She desires that the Lord may bless benevolent Boaz, for she recognizes Boaz's extraordinary act of grace. "Mara's" tone has changed!

But whose "kindness has not forsaken the living or the dead"? Grammatically in the original Hebrew this could refer to either Yahweh or Boaz. It may be deliberately ambiguous, since both the Lord's and Boaz's actions could accurately be described as being characterized by *hesed*. Boaz's actions are above and beyond what is strictly required. His actions involve generosity to and sacrifice for one who is in need: Ruth. Thus, he displays biblical *hesed*. But of course the Lord is showing his steadfast love and faithfulness throughout the narrative too. He is at work, providing and showing kindness in addition to empowering Boaz for such action.

There are two primary reasons for thinking that the "who" in fact refers to Yahweh. First, the term "the man" is used in **verse 20b** ("The man is a close relative") instead of "he." It would seem unnecessary to say "the man" if Naomi were continuing to speak of Boaz—"he" would make more sense. So it seems that she was referring to the Lord's kindness and then shifted to talking about

Boaz, marking the change with the words "the man." Second, a similar statement is made in Genesis 24:27 which obviously refers to Yahweh: "Blessed be the LORD, the God of my master Abraham, who has not forsaken his steadfast love and his faithfulness toward my master. As for me, the LORD has led me in the way to the house of my master's kinsmen."

This is the point: God has been kind to Naomi and Ruth. We are seeing here what we may call Naomi's personal revival. Her view of the Almighty is being restored. Her bitterness is being replaced by thankfulness. By saying that the Lord has not forsaken "the living or the dead," she seems to be saying that the Lord is showing kindness and faithfulness to her whole family—to her and to Ruth, both widows of deceased husbands—and she seems to be hinting at her future hope: the hope that Ruth and Boaz may be married and have a son. This hope will become clearer when we understand the concept of the redeemer. But for now, as Block concludes, "This speech represents a total turnaround from her despairing and accusatory words in [Ruth] 1:20-21" (*Judges, Ruth*, page 673). There Naomi saw only bitterness in her situation; now she recognizes that the Lord's kindness has never forsaken her.

If you are in a season of grief, allow Naomi's turnaround to encourage you. *Weeping may last for a night, but joy comes in the morning,* as the psalmist says (Psalm 30:5, my paraphrase). By God's grace, it is possible to go from "mourning" to "dancing" (Psalm 30:11).

Hope for the Future

Naomi next gives her second response to Ruth: "The man is a close relative of ours, one of our redeemers" (Ruth **2:20**). Naomi's mind must have been racing at this point! For Boaz was more than a good-hearted Israelite. The Hebrew word *go'el* ("redeemer") is significant. It means a "kinsman-redeemer": a close relative who is able to come to the aid of a family member. This concept is introduced here and will be developed in chapter 3.

In one sense, Boaz has already acted as a *go'el* by providing for Ruth and Naomi. But Naomi has more in mind, because she knows what God's law says about the role of a redeemer.

Leviticus 25:25-55 outlines specific ways in which a redeemer could protect and help his relatives. If someone became poor and had to sell their property, a close kinsman—"his nearest redeemer" (v 25)—was to buy it back on their behalf. If someone fell into slavery, then being their redeemer meant buying them back from their owners (v 47-49) and treating them kindly (v 39-40, 53). A redeemer could be a brother, uncle, cousin, or other close relative (v 48-49).

Related to this, and more relevant to Ruth, are the commands in Deuteronomy 25:5-10 about levirate marriage. The instructions were that when a man died, his brother was obliged to marry his widow and raise up his children. He was even to give the dead man's name to the first child born out of the new marriage. This would ensure that the inheritance would continue to be associated with the deceased relative.

The situation in *Ruth* does not precisely match the provisions in Leviticus and Deuteronomy. First, Naomi and Ruth were not in debt or enslaved. They were poor, but they did not need to be bought back from anyone. Further, although Ruth was a widow, the law did not address the question of what obligations, if any, a kinsman-redeemer had toward foreigners, who were not supposed to have married into the family in the first place. It is not certain that Ruth would have expected a relative of her husband to marry her after she was widowed.

Second, Boaz was not a brother to Mahlon and Chilion, nor to Elimelech. He was a family relative, part of the same clan, which meant that he had the right to act as a redeemer if he chose, but he was not obliged to do so in the way that a brother would have been. Notice that Naomi says Boaz is "one of our redeemers"; he's not the only redeemer (Ruth **2:20**; see also 4:1, 3, 6, 8). She seems to know of another closer redeemer. Later, Boaz confirms the existence of a closer relative (3:12-13). Whoever could redeem the widow or poor relation was to do so, but the greater responsibility fell to the nearest relative. Naomi's statement about Boaz recognizes his connection and obligation but also implies that there is another potential husband for Ruth.

So there were plenty of excuses Boaz could make in order to be absolved of responsibility toward Ruth and Naomi. But Boaz, as we have seen, is a man of grace, not a man who looks for loopholes or the minimum requirements. He will be motivated not merely by the law but by love.

The skies are turning bluer for Naomi. Boaz's provision for her through Ruth and his relationship to her as a relative have changed her disposition. In chapter 3, we will see that she has a lot in mind for Ruth and Boaz!

> A man of grace is motivated not merely by the law but by love.

In **2:21**, after reminding us again that Ruth is a "Moabite," the narrator records her response to Naomi. Ruth restates Boaz's words to her: "You shall keep close by my young men until they have finished all my harvest." Boaz did more than grant her a "day of grace." His special treatment would continue. Naomi is greatly pleased by Boaz's ongoing provision in allowing Ruth gleaning privileges throughout the harvest season. She encourages Ruth to press on: "It is good, my daughter, that you go out with his young women, lest in another field you be assaulted" (**v 22**). Naomi's statement highlights how extraordinary Boaz's treatment of Ruth is: in any other field she would be in danger of being assaulted. Naomi's concern for Ruth's safety is one she shares with Boaz.

The chapter concludes with Ruth staying close to Boaz's young women, gleaning until the end of the barley and wheat harvests, and continuing to live with her mother-in-law (**v 23**). But the romantic reader may see the chapter ending on a downer. After the completion of the harvests, nothing is said of any potential relationship between Boaz and Ruth—nor of any other plan for future provision.

Ruth would have been in regular contact with Boaz for these six to seven weeks, yet nothing is said of their relationship developing. Now the harvest season is over, and Ruth is still living with her mother-in-law. She is still a widow at the end of chapter 2. We must wait for the next chapter to see how things progress between her and Boaz. Before we do, however, we are going to look more carefully at the concept of the redeemer.

Questions for reflection

1. How could you exemplify *hesed* like Boaz? In what specific ways could you show generosity and compassion at work, at church, or at home?

2. What difficult "Naomis" could you reach out to or pray for this week?

3. God gave the laws about redeemers mentioned on page 84. What does that suggest about his character?

1) - Be more like Ellen!
- Make a bigger effort with all staff
- In how I speak to the kids

2) - Ruth
- Valerie

3) - Loving father, providing & protecting, importance of family in canny

PART TWO

Looking Through Boaz: Christ our Redeemer

The concept of redemption is central to the story of the Bible. The Bible is a unified book of redemptive history, which culminates in Christ. The book of *Ruth* contributes to our understanding of redemption by giving us a concrete example of it. The story draws our attention to the various aspects involved in redemption and points ahead to the greater Redeemer, Christ, increasing our affections for him.

Since we have just now been introduced to Boaz as a "redeemer," a theme developed in the next two chapters of *Ruth*, a consideration of this biblical mega-theme is fitting at this point. We need to consider four aspects of redemption in *Ruth* and across the biblical storyline:

1. the need for redemption

2. the price of redemption

3. the glory of the redeemer

4. the familial nature of redemption

While each example of redemption in the Bible has unique features, they bear these resemblances. These elements of redemption converge on Christ, as the theme develops toward the New Testament.

The Need for Redemption

We need redemption because we are weak and helpless. All examples of redemption in the Bible include this element. In *Ruth*, the need is for food and family. Ruth and Naomi are vulnerable widows in a patriarchal society. They need provision now, and they need security for the future. They cannot solve this problem on their own: they need a redeemer. A husband and a child for Ruth will end the crisis, provide for their needs, and continue their family line.

In other cases of redemption, too, powerlessness is clearly observable. In the exodus, the people of Israel were enslaved in Egypt. They were desperate. They could not free themselves. They were under political slavery, ruled by a foreign power (Exodus 1:8-10). They were under economic slavery (1:11-14), ruthlessly made to work. They were under social slavery (1:15-22), under a pharaoh's state-sponsored genocide that demanded the killing of all male Hebrew babies. Finally, they were under spiritual slavery: God desired to deliver them so that "they may worship [him]" (9:1, CSB). The story goes on to show that even when the people had got out of Egypt, Egypt was still in them! In their hearts, they often longed to return to Egypt (Acts 7:39). Israel desperately needed freedom (Exodus 2:23). God knew this. He said to his people, "I will redeem you with an outstretched arm and with great acts of judgment" (6:6).

Following the exodus, God gave his people laws which expressed his heart for the needy; he made provisions for the weak. Leviticus 25 is an important chapter on freedom from bondage. Various laws regarding the **Sabbath year** (Leviticus 25:1-7), the **jubilee** (v 8-22), redeeming land and houses (v 23-34), redeeming the poor and maintaining freedom (v 35-46), and redeeming those in **indentured service** (v 47-54) are described. As we have already seen, the kinsman redeemer was to act on behalf of relatives who needed redemption. God's law outlined all of these situations and made provision for those who were weak and helpless.

Later Israel would be under another foreign power: Babylon. God's people would again experience a similar slavery. They would need God to intervene and free them. Jeremiah envisioned the redemption of Israel and Judah from an oppressor that had "hands too strong for him" (Jeremiah 31:11). Isaiah said that, in the end, **Zion** would be saved and be called "the Redeemed of the LORD" (Isaiah 62:12).

In the Psalms, weakness is often expressed as an individual cry for redemption. The psalmists cry out to God because of all sorts of danger: trouble, affliction, shame, the threat of death, and more. God is presented as the Redeemer, who comes to rescue the needy (Psalm 18; 25:19-22; 72:12-14; 77; 103:4; 107).

In the New Testament, the need and helplessness of every one of us is clear. We are dead in sin and in need of new life (Ephesians 2:1-3; John 11). We are slaves to sin (Romans 5:12; 6:16-20, 23), unable to free ourselves and unable to serve God as we ought (Galatians 5:1, 13-15). We are alienated from God, having no fellowship with God (Ephesians 2:12-21). We are under the wrath of God, needing salvation by the grace of God (Ephesians 2:1-10). We are in the kingdom of darkness, needing to be transferred into the kingdom of light (Colossians 1:13-14). We are spiritually hungry, needing the living water and the bread of life for satisfaction (John 4; 6 – 7). We are blind, unable to see the truth of God and the glory of the Messiah (John 9). We are lost sheep, needing the Good Shepherd to rescue us (John 10).

The great tragedy today is that many do not see their need for salvation. It is easy for people to see Ruth's need for a husband, and very easy to understand Israel's need in Egypt, but many are blind to their own need for spiritual redemption. It has been said that to become a Christian, "all you need is need"; but not everyone recognizes their need for Christ the Redeemer.

The Price of Redemption

This element will generate more discussion in Ruth 3 – 4. If we glance ahead, we find that the kinsman who is more closely related to Naomi than Boaz has to consider the cost of redemption (4:1-6). He is invited to act as a redeemer and buy back Elimelech's property, and is willing to do so; but when he hears that he will need to marry Ruth, too, he is no longer willing. The price is too great. It would be a challenge, for example, to meet the cost of feeding Ruth, Naomi, and future children. In an agrarian society, this would have brought additional burdens and risk on the rest of the family. If they fell into poverty, the result would have been that they would become slaves or bond-servants. But Boaz was willing to pay the price, as Ruth 3 – 4 will show. He was willing to pay to redeem the property of Elimelech, and he was willing to take the risk of marrying Ruth.

In the exodus, the deliverance from Egypt was bound up with the Passover lamb. In order to be rescued from Egypt, and from God's judgment on Egypt, the Israelites had to sacrifice a lamb and daub the blood on their doorframes. Only those who were under the blood of the lamb would be saved (Exodus 12:3-13). Again, redemption had a price, though in this case the ones being redeemed were making the payment of a precious lamb. The Passover-lamb event becomes a major theme in the New Testament, when Jesus Christ is heralded as the Lamb of God, who ultimately takes away the sin of the world through the payment of his own life and blood (John 1:29).

Further, in the Old Testament laws, redemption often happened through a commercial transaction. A kinsman had to make a payment to redeem property and slaves (Leviticus 25:25-33, 48-51).

In the New Testament, as mentioned previously, this theme develops. Paul says we were "bought with a price" (1 Corinthians 6:20; 7:23). We have freedom from bondage through the death of Jesus, the greater Passover lamb (1 Corinthians 5:7). **Atoning** blood was shed to purchase our freedom. Jesus' death is the ransom paid for us (Mark 10:45). Peter says we have been redeemed not with silver or gold, but by the precious blood of Christ (1 Peter 1:18-19). We could cite more references, all the way to Revelation, where Jesus is worshiped as the Lamb who was slain for sinners from every tribe and tongue (Revelation 5:9).

The Glory of the Redeemer

How could Jesus' death pay the price for so many people? Knowing the nature of a redeemer is important for answering this question. To be a redeemer you had to have both the willingness and the ability to redeem. When it came to Ruth's redemption, Boaz had both. He was a man of both moral worth and material wealth. He demonstrated the character of a redeemer through his selfless actions. He looked out for the powerless and the weak. He reflected God's *hesed*: his kindness, loyalty, mercy, and faithfulness. His status as a landowner also demonstrated the fact that he had the financial capacity to become a redeemer.

God's redeeming work throughout the Old Testament may likewise be observed through his willingness and his ability, his character and his power. God was willing to hear the cries of Israel, and able to deliver them from the world superpower, Egypt. After freeing his people, the Lord then issued instructions in his law to show his people how to reflect his character. They were to show grace to the sojourner because they themselves had once been strangers in the land of Egypt before the Lord brought them out (Leviticus 19:33; Deuteronomy 10:19). God's heart for redemption was to be expressed through his people, who were to care for the widow, the orphan, and the stranger. Further, they were to release slaves, since God had rescued them from slavery in Egypt (Deuteronomy 15:12-15). The ways in which a redeemer may release his family members, listed in Leviticus 25, are, as Lau and Goswell say, "like mini-exoduses" (*Unceasing Kindness*, page 130).

The nature of Christ our Redeemer is evidenced in both his willingness to redeem and his ability to do it. His willingness is described in various places, such as Philippians 2:6-8: he "emptied himself, by taking the form of a servant ... he humbled himself." Jesus' selfless love stimulates profound gratitude in the heart of the redeemed. His kindness and grace are demonstrated in his life and his death for sinners. Jesus is also able to redeem. His ability to redeem goes beyond that of Boaz; Christ came to redeem not just one person, not even just Israel, but the nations. How can his death atone for so many? Because of his own immeasurable worth. Because of his own glory—being equal with the Father—his atonement has immeasurable value.

The Familial Nature of Redemption

Throughout Scripture the concept of redemption is inherently bound up with the realm of family. This is certainly the case with Ruth and Boaz, as Boaz, a relative and redeemer, becomes Ruth's husband and extends the family line. Thus, we see redemption leading to intimacy, relationship, and family.

> **Throughout Scripture, redemption leads to intimacy, relationship, and family.**

The same is true for the exodus. God's redemption is explained with familial language. God is the ultimate *go'el* who redeems his people. He calls Israel his "son" (Exodus 4:23). When his "relatives" were in bonded labor and spiritual slavery, he came to intervene, avenge, and rescue them. God encourages a discouraged Moses by reminding him of this promise of redemption (6:5-6). He then tells Moses of the purpose or goal of that redemption: "I will take you to be my people, and I will be your God, and you shall know that I am the LORD your God" (6:7; note that this statement is echoed in Ruth's **confession** of faith, Ruth 1:16). Thus, redemption and covenant relationship are tied together— the redemption of the Passover is "just the start of the divine plan to redeem a family for himself" (Lau and Goswell, *Unceasing Kindness*, page 133). Further, God also uses the language of "inheritance" with Moses (Exodus 6:8): a particular land given to his people.

This link between redemption and familial language continues throughout the Old Testament. Isaiah describes God as "maker," "husband," and "redeemer" in one verse (Isaiah 54:5), and later uses "father" and "redeemer" in one verse (63:16).

In the cases of Ruth and of Israel, the relational bonds grow tighter after redemption. In Exodus God redeems his people, and then the relational bonds are deepened. In *Ruth*, Boaz and Ruth's relationship involves increased relational unity: they get married and begin a family.

Boaz, we will see, will fulfill the role of a kinsman-redeemer by buying Naomi's field and marrying her daughter-in-law. Ruth, who has taken refuge under the wings of the Almighty, is recognized by Boaz as part of God's people and brought into Boaz's own family.

In the New Testament, redemption continues to look like marriage. The church is the bride of Christ; Paul says that the union of our first parents—and other marriages, like Ruth and Boaz's marriage—mysteriously points to Jesus' relationship with his bride, the church (Ephesians 5:28-33). However, there is also another familial image that is used to describe what it is like to be redeemed by Christ. The redeemed are the adopted: Christians become the children of God—brothers and sisters in God's household:

> "When the fullness of time had come, God sent forth his Son, born of woman, born under the law, to redeem those who were under the law, so that we might receive adoption as sons. And because you are sons, God has sent the Spirit of his Son into our hearts, crying, '**Abba**! Father!' So you are no longer a slave, but a son, and if a son, then an heir through God." (Galatians 4:4-7)

Notice the double purpose: "to redeem … so that we might receive adoption."

This passage reminds us again that we need redemption; we were crushed under the law and enslaved (v 5, 7; see also v 8). We could not keep God's law, and we could not set ourselves free. But Christ has redeemed us by paying a price: "by becoming a curse for us" (3:13). Adoption is free for the one who is adopted, but costly for the one who adopts. It cost Jesus his life and his death—he came from heaven to live the human life we could never have lived, keeping God's law perfectly, and he died the death we should have died.

Paul also stresses Jesus' unique nature: the Father "sent forth his Son," but the Son was also "born of woman" (4:4). Jesus is both fully divine and fully man, yet in one person. He is of infinite worth. Jesus is the one and only God-man: the only One able to redeem sinful humanity. He was also willing to redeem, as evidenced by his completed mission, which led to the sending of the "Spirit" (v 6).

And so the familial nature of redemption is beautifully displayed in this concept of adoption (see also Romans 8:12-30; Ephesians 1:3-14). We are sons and daughters of God through our redemption by Christ

Jesus. This has also provided us with an inheritance. We will inherit a new heaven and a new earth (Matthew 5:5), and most importantly of all, we have God himself as our inheritance (Psalm 73:25). We enjoy some of this inheritance now but look forward to our full enjoyment of it later. This relationship has given us greater intimacy than could be had in the Old Testament, because the Holy Spirit indwells us (Galatians 4:6), confirming our adoption (Romans 8:14, 16) and enabling us to say, "Abba, Father" (Galatians 4:6; Romans 8:15)—that is, we have the privilege of communing with God all the time.

When we look at Boaz, we see many godly traits to imitate. But when we look through Boaz, we see the gospel of Jesus Christ. Jesus sees us in our need, pays the price for our redemption, gives us a new status, and brings us into the most intimate of relationships. How do we respond to such grace? Ruth's response to Boaz (Ruth 2:10) points in the right direction: to fall before our Redeemer and worship the One who has shown us *hesed*. In the last chapter, we saw how we could follow the example of Boaz to serve the poor and powerless. Now, as we understand how Boaz is a picture of a greater Redeemer, we can worship our Savior, the One who has redeemed us and who now empowers us to serve.

Questions for reflection

1. Who could you pray for who is in need of salvation?

2. Think of someone you want to share the gospel with. Do they most need to understand their need of redemption, the price it cost, the glorious nature of Jesus the Redeemer, or the family they would be redeemed into?

3. What could you say or do to encourage other Christians to worship and to serve God?

6. THE THRESHING FLOOR

"What a man, what a man, what a mighty good man!" So begins the 1993 Salt-N-Pepa pop song. While I don't endorse (or remember) every line from this song, this catchy line expressed a basic idea shared by many women: the value of finding a respectable man. Many continue to repeat the familiar phrase "A good man is hard to find." It is true today, and it was true in the days of Ruth.

In Ruth 2, we met a mighty good man—Boaz. He was described as a "worthy man" (2:1): a man of substance (both materially and morally). He was single, a potential redeemer, and a man of mercy and justice. He lavished kindness on Ruth and her mother-in-law, and Naomi recognized that he could be a redeemer for them, marrying Ruth. But chapter 2 finishes with a downer. There is no date between Ruth and Boaz. We want to see Boaz ask Ruth out, but chapter 2 just leaves us hanging! We are left to wonder: will anything happen between these two?

Today, there are many ways in which singles try to connect with other singles online. Ruth did not have this option. A "Bethlehem Bachelor" TV show did not exist; she could not even run an ad in the newspaper, and if she could have done, who would have been interested in a woman who came with her mother-in-law in tow?

Naomi, though, devises a plan (**3:1-5**). It will lead to Ruth's proposal to Boaz (v 6-9). Boaz will respond with a promise to Ruth (v 10-13), and by providing for her (v 14-18). Pay attention to the time of these events: Naomi devises her plan in the evening; Ruth makes her move around midnight; and Boaz's provision and Naomi's evaluation of things happen the next morning. The times say something about the kind of story we are about to read—one filled with suspense. We read these events like a movie in which time slows down in view of the risk and the possible consequences of Ruth's actions.

Before we look at these four stages—the plan, proposal, promise, and provision—it is important to remember a few things. First, a basic rule in biblical interpretation is that narratives are not always normative. Not everything in a story is something we should attempt to do! Narrators are simply describing events, not necessarily prescribing activities. As a father of three teenage daughters, I cringe at the idea of giving Naomi's counsel to them! We must always allow all of Scripture to help us draw appropriate principles from stories. To be sure, there are applications to make from this story, but we must make them wisely, with all of Scripture in view. Second, this story is full of suspense and not every detail is explained fully. The narrator does not tell us everything, and there are some cultural practices that we simply do not fully understand. We are left with many questions after reading this story, but we must focus attention on what is clear and applicable, and avoid making dominant points from speculations. Third, the sensuality in the story will make some uncomfortable, but this very tension is important because it highlights the purity of both Ruth and Boaz. Other Old Testament stories in similar settings led to sexual immorality (Genesis 19:31-3; 38:1-30), but both Boaz and Ruth give us a much-needed example of godliness—in a time in which "everyone did what was right in his own eyes" (Judges 21:25).

Naomi's Plan

The story begins with the rejuvenated Naomi expressing her desire to find Ruth a husband (Ruth **3:1**). Instead of being self-absorbed, Naomi is now looking out for Ruth's welfare—a sign that God's *hesed* is melting Naomi's cold heart. Naomi longs for her daughter-in-law to settle down and find peace, protection, and provision through marriage.

Naomi's plan involves Ruth initiating a meeting with Boaz. Once again, we see that even though the book of Ruth highlights the providence of God, the characters do not slip into passive **fatalism**. They are active, not disengaged. Naomi does not say, *God is sovereign, so let's just wait until a husband knocks on the door!* God's sovereignty is not a license for human inactivity. That would be not trusting the Lord but testing the Lord. No, we should work and act, in view of and because of God's work and God's activity.

> God's sovereignty is not a license for human inactivity. That is not trusting the Lord but testing the Lord.

Naomi reminds Ruth that Boaz is a relative (**v 2**) and informs her that he will be "winnowing barley tonight" at the threshing floor. It is striking that Naomi knew this bit of information. How did she receive it? We do not know, but Naomi had apparently done some research. Previously, Naomi prayed for the Lord to provide a husband and "rest" (1:8-9), but now she seeks an opportunity to answer her own prayer! She seizes an opportunity that the Lord has provided.

The threshing floor (**3:2**) was the place where farmers would winnow, separating grain from chaff after all the grain had been gathered. Farmers would toss a mixture of straw, grain, and chaff in the air with a pitchfork. The heavier kernels of grain would fall to the ground, while the chaff—the unwanted husk around the kernel—would be blown away. The winnowing, or threshing, usually occurred at night because night breezes were needed for this separation. The location was often a hilltop, which was also better for breezes. It was usually done on a hard surface such as rock, so that the grain would not mix with dust and the chaff could be easily blown away. These threshing floors were communal places, often shared by members of the village, and were places of joy and celebration because the work of threshing meant that the harvest had come in. The workers would sleep in these locations in order to protect their grain. While the threshing floor was a place associated with immoral behavior, including prostitution (Hosea 9:1), Naomi sees this as the right opportunity for Ruth to have a special meeting with Boaz, despite the dangerous nature of this setting. She clearly has a high view of Boaz.

Naomi provides specific instructions for Ruth (Ruth **3:3-4**). She proposes seven steps.

1. Take a bath (**v 3**). This is always good advice when pursuing a spouse!

2. Put on some perfume. Scented oils were common at this time, and helpful given the fact that modern deodorants did not exist. Oil was also a sign of abundance and luxury (as in Psalm 23:5 or Mark 14:3). Ruth needs to make an effort.

3. Put on some fresh clothes (Ruth **3:3**). Ruth must no longer look like a widow in a time of mourning. (Compare 2 Samuel 12:20, where David performs these same three steps as a sign that he is no longer mourning.) Naomi's goal is not only to make Ruth look and smell alluring—but her plan does include this aspect. This is a helpful corrective for those who condemn paying attention to physical appearance. Of course character is more important than looks (1 Peter 3:3-4; Proverbs 31:30), but Christians are not Gnostics (people who downplay physical things and only emphasize spiritual things). The Bible does not avoid saying that people and things in creation may be pleasing to the eye and the other senses (Genesis 39:6b; Ecclesiastes 11:7; Song of Songs 1:2-3; 4:1-7; Matthew 6:28-29). We are not to worship the way we look, or find our confidence or security in it; but we need not flee from caring about our appearance.

4. Visit Boaz at the threshing floor when he is in a good mood. Trying to get something out of someone who is hungry is never a very good idea! It is always better to wait until they are full before discussing something significant. So Ruth is to wait until he "has finished eating and drinking" (Ruth **3:3**). After a hard

day's work, and some good food and a sip of wine, Boaz will be relaxed. There have been years of famine, but now we can imagine Boaz staring up at the stars, under the blessing of God, feeling very happy. Sure enough, in verse 7 we are told that "his heart was merry."

This picture of Boaz is important. Some people seem to believe that to pursue a life of holiness we must abandon all pleasure. But that is not the case. Delight in God and gratitude toward God is the heart condition of a holy person. It's a matter of finding your ultimate pleasure in God: the God who gives us everything for our enjoyment (1 Timothy 6:17) and in whom lies far greater pleasure than anything humans can offer. This is why Ephesians 5:18 instructs us, "Do not get drunk with wine … but be filled with the Spirit." Boaz did not get drunk but enjoyed God's gifts rightly. We, too, should labor, eat, drink, rest, and enjoy creation in such a way that the Giver of such gifts is glorified. We sin when we exchange the Creator for his gifts in creation (Romans 1:25). We sin when we enjoy the gifts but do not praise the Giver. We also sin when we demean or decry those gifts, for that does not praise the Giver either (1 Timothy 4:1-5). Like Boaz, we are to enjoy them properly, as God designed, with gratitude and for his glory.

5. Observe where Boaz lies down (Ruth **3:4**). Ruth definitely needs to follow this step; make sure it is Boaz!

6. Uncover Boaz's feet and lie down close to him. We can sense the tension in these instructions. The purpose of such a sensual gesture is intended to communicate something to Boaz. Apparently, this nonverbal gesture was a customary means of requesting marriage (see Hubbard, *The Book of Ruth,* page 221)—something that Ruth will eventually communicate verbally.

7. Listen to Boaz's instructions. Naomi says, "He will tell you what to do." Naomi trustingly leaves the matter to Boaz. She has made her plans, but the Lord will determine the next steps (Proverbs 16:9).

In Ruth **3:5**, we read of Ruth's remarkable commitment to the plan: "All that you say I will do." We see Ruth's loyalty to Naomi here, as well as her courage.

Naomi has devised quite a scheme. We do not read of this specific method anywhere else in Scripture. Since Naomi has identified Boaz as a redeemer, she clearly thinks Ruth's chances of marriage are increased by his relationship to the family. But the harvest time has gone by, and Boaz has not made a move. So Naomi wants to encourage him to act. No other redeemer has acted yet either. Why not? Was Boaz waiting on the closer relative to act? Was it because Ruth was a Moabite? Were they keeping their distance because Ruth was grieving? Did Boaz simply think Ruth was out of his league (see v 10)? Whatever the case, Ruth's actions at the threshing floor will force Boaz to say and do something.

This is a risky plan. Many men in this situation could respond in a variety of negative ways. If groggy, Boaz could respond harshly— "What are you doing! I just fell asleep!" He could also charge Ruth with acting like a prostitute—coming to him at the threshing floor in the dead of night—and shame her publicly. Most significant is the threat of sexual violence. It is possible that Boaz may interpret Ruth's actions as a license to sin; for it seems most men in the period of the judges would have justified abuse or sexual sin in this situation. The danger of such violence has already been mentioned twice in the narrative: Boaz warned his workers not to touch Ruth (2:9), and Naomi told her to stay away from other fields where she might be assaulted (2:22). If working in broad daylight in the open fields was a danger to Ruth, how much more dangerous would it be to go out alone in the middle of the night and lie down beside a man! If Boaz wanted to assault Ruth, he could do so very easily. There are great risks. As Naomi gives these instructions and as Ruth wholeheartedly accepts them, they are both displaying enormous trust in Boaz's integrity.

So there are aspects of this plan that we would not recommend to our daughters! But the riskiness of the strategy Naomi commends to

Ruth serves to expose the one thing that will make it secure: Boaz. If Naomi has overestimated his kindness, integrity, and status as a close family member, the plan will go seriously wrong. The plan all depends upon Boaz and on him alone.

The same is true for us as Christian believers. As we make plans—as we try to figure out strategies for ministry and make good decisions in our lives—we know that there is one person on whom everything depends: the Lord Jesus. We are called to live in such a way that everything depends on the kindness, integrity, and redeeming power of the Lord Jesus. To the extent that we know we can trust him, we will take risks to live for him and to further his kingdom. When we hold back and play safe, we are often betraying a small view of Jesus: a suspicion deep down that he may not come through for us, that he cannot be trusted to do what is best for us. When we see him as he is—the perfect Boaz, a redeemer and bridegroom of perfect kindness and integrity—then we can joyfully lean on his character, living in a way that only makes sense because he is who he is.

Questions for reflection

1. What do Naomi's words suggest about her attitude to Ruth, to Boaz, and to God?

2. How can you express trust in Jesus in the way you make and talk about your decisions?

3. What risks could you take to further Christ's kingdom?

PART TWO

Ruth's Proposal

The plan has been hatched; and now Ruth goes to the threshing floor, "just as her mother-in-law had commanded her" (Ruth **3:6**). She waits until Boaz's heart is "merry," having finished his meal (**v 7**). She observes where he lays down, and then she quietly enters: "She came softly and uncovered his feet and lay down." We can feel the tension as Boaz feels the air on his feet...

Put yourself in Boaz's sandals. How would you react in this situation? You have put in a full day of work. You have eaten well and thanked God for his gifts in creation. Now you are enjoying some rest amid the grain provided by the Lord. All is well. And then you wake up with cold feet! What is more, you find a woman lying next to you (**v 8**)! The amazement is communicated with the word "behold." Understandably, in the dark he asks this woman, "Who are you?" (**v 9**). We do not know how he asked this question. Did he whisper? Did he react in a sense of shock and surprise? Was he upset?

Ruth answers briefly: "I am Ruth, your servant." Her response is different from 2:13, where she was amazed at Boaz's favor, given that she was not one of his servants. Now she is identifying herself as having an improved status; she is the kind of woman that Boaz might marry.

Ruth does not follow Naomi's plan exactly. Instead of waiting on Boaz's instructions, Ruth takes the initiative. She is essentially proposing to Boaz when she says, "Spread your wings over your servant, for you are a redeemer" (**3:9**). She communicates her desires to him. She is not interested in some dirty one-night stand. She is interested in marriage—the idiom "spread your wings" (or "garment") elsewhere is an idiom for marriage (see Ezekiel 16:8). Boaz also used this expression previously to describe how Ruth sought refuge under the wings of Yahweh (Ruth 2:12). Now Ruth is asking Boaz to become part of God's protection and provision for her life.

With the phrase "you are a redeemer" (**3:9**), Ruth reminds Boaz of his relationship to the family and the opportunity to come to their aid. But there is also some caution expressed here. Boaz is "a redeemer" but not the only redeemer: he is not the closest family member. Nor was Boaz was the brother of Elimelech, nor of his sons. Remember, under certain circumstances, the kinsman-redeemer was obligated to marry his brother's widow in order to raise up for the dead brother a family who could inherit his property (Deuteronomy 25:5-10). But Boaz was not in this precise position. He did have a family connection with Naomi and Ruth, so it was possible for him to act in the spirit of the law and become a redeemer. But we must not think that Boaz had no choice in this matter. He was not the brother. Otherwise, this whole midnight drama would have been unnecessary. Ruth could just have gone up and asked him to marry her in the daylight, appealing to the law.

In other words, the fact that Boaz was "a redeemer" did not mean that the marriage was a done deal. But Ruth raises the issue because she thinks it increases her chances with Boaz, and because she knows something of the character of Boaz; he is willing to follow the spirit of the law, not just its minimum requirements. Boaz's redeemer status also implied that he could help support Naomi—since it was her husband he was related to—and indeed Boaz does display concern for Ruth's mother-in-law in the story.

Ruth continues to amaze us. Block summarizes her proposal:

"Here is a servant demanding that the boss marry her, a Moabite making the demand of an Israelite, a woman making the demand of a man, a poor person making the demand of a rich man. Was this an act of foreigner naïveté, or a daughter-in-law's devotion to her mother-in-law, or another sign of the hidden hand of God? From a natural perspective the scheme was doomed from the beginning as a hopeless gamble, and the responsibility Naomi placed on Ruth was quite unreasonable. But it worked!"

(*Judges, Ruth*, page 692)

It was indeed a bold move by a bold Moabite!

Boaz's Promise

Before giving Ruth a direct answer to her proposal, Boaz blesses Ruth. It turns out that he is not put off by her directness but pleased by it: "May you be blessed by the LORD, my daughter. You have made this last kindness greater than the first in that you have not gone after young men, whether poor or rich" (Ruth **3:10**). Boaz was impressed before (2:11) by Ruth's kindness toward Naomi in choosing to journey to Bethlehem with her. Now the "kindness" (*hesed*) referred to is Ruth's desire to provide Naomi with an heir by marrying Boaz.

Added to this is Boaz's delight that Ruth has not "gone after other young men, whether poor or rich" (**3:10**). Based upon this statement, it seems safe to assume that Ruth is younger than Boaz (who refers to her as "my daughter," not only here but also in **verse 11** and 2:8). We should not think of Boaz as some frail old man; he has demonstrated a robust work ethic. But he is older than Ruth, and it also seems that Ruth is more attractive than Boaz. She could have gone after young men (or, literally, "choice men"), but she has decided not to pursue a guy out of greed (the "rich"), nor out of attraction and passion (the "poor")—this is a hint that she was capable of gaining either because of her own youthful attractiveness. Instead Ruth has other values, such as family loyalty.

Stepping back for a moment, we are left to marvel at the purity of both Boaz and Ruth. Instead of engaging in some steamy sexual encounter, Boaz praises Yahweh for Ruth! Nor does Ruth make any sexual advances toward Boaz in an effort to win him.

In **3:11**, Boaz comforts Ruth by saying, "Do not fear." We can imagine how fast Ruth's heart must have been beating—this is the crucial moment of decision. And Boaz promises to do everything that she has requested, which probably includes taking care of the family and property, not just marrying Ruth. Boaz also notes that all his fellow townsmen recognize Ruth as a "worthy woman"—a phrase which also occurs in Proverbs 31:10, where it is translated in the ESV as "excellent wife." Another connection to Proverbs 31 is the fact that all of Boaz's fellow townsmen esteem Ruth (Ruth **3:11**)—as Proverbs 31:31 puts it, "Her works praise her in the gates." Ruth is a Proverbs 31 woman, who is respected and praised by others. Her ultimate beauty is her godliness.

But, just as the happy ending seems secured, Boaz raises a problem: there is an unnamed man who is a closer relative than him (Ruth **3:12**). The happy ending is put on hold: "Remain tonight," Boaz tells Ruth, "and in the morning, if he will redeem you, good; let him do it. But if he is not willing to redeem you, then, as the LORD lives, I will redeem you. Lie down until the morning" (**v 13**). The other relative has a more legitimate claim than Boaz, and Boaz honors this social custom. But Boaz pledges under God that if the other man is unwilling to redeem Ruth, he himself will marry her. Either way, Ruth will have a redeemer. Boaz then urges Ruth to remain with him during the night for the purpose of safety (nothing in the text indicates any kind of sinful activity overnight). Ruth will not have to approach this other relative directly, for Boaz will address him personally the next day.

Boaz's Provision

In the morning, before he approaches the other redeemer at the city gate, Boaz extends grace once again to Ruth and Naomi. Before it is light enough for people to recognize Ruth, Boaz sends her home (**v 14**). This early send-off is meant to preserve her dignity and reputation— things that obviously matter to Boaz.

He sends Ruth off with a gift. Telling her to hold out her garment, he proceeds to put six measures of barley in it (**v 15**). The nature of this garment is uncertain. But no doubt it is very large and made of very sturdy material, since it is able to hold a large amount of grain. It is such a large amount, in fact, that Boaz has to "put it on her," either on her head, on her back, or over her back: an amount that was most likely around 60-90 pounds (30-40 kg) of grain. She then carries it all the way home!

This generous provision of food seems to have been provided for at least three reasons. First, it was a means of basic provision for two desperate widows. Second, it would have explained why Ruth had been at Boaz's threshing floor, should anyone have seen her leaving. Third, and most significantly, it was a symbolic provision—a message to Naomi.

The nature of that message becomes clear as Naomi and Ruth discuss the threshing-floor encounter in **verses 16-17**. When Ruth returns, Naomi is eager to hear about Ruth's status. The ESV reads, "How did you fare, my daughter?" (**v 16**). But that is not a literal translation; she actually asks, "Who are you, my daughter?" It is the same question Boaz asked Ruth in **verse 9**. Of course Naomi knows who Ruth is. What she wants to know is: is Ruth still a Moabite widow or has her status changed? Remember, previously Boaz asked, "Whose young woman is this?" and the foreman responded, "She is the young Moabite woman, who came back with Naomi" (2:6). Is this still Ruth's status? Naomi is essentially asking, *Did the plan work? Are you going to be his wife? Has everything turned around for us?*

Ruth tells Naomi everything that Boaz has done. Then she mentions the grain: "These six measures of barley he gave to me, for he said to me, 'You must not go back empty-handed to your mother-in-law'" (**3:17**). Ruth includes something that the narrator did not previously include. Boaz's gift was intended to bless Naomi. Boaz is serious about his pursuit of Ruth—so serious that this will involve caring for her mother-in-law too. To symbolize this, he provides this extravagant gift.

> We are witnessing Naomi's journey from emptiness to fullness.

This same Naomi once described herself as "empty" (1:21). Then, she was both childless and hungry; now, she has a full load of grain before her. Boaz's gift is probably symbolic of both kinds of provision. Grain may be meant to symbolize offspring. We are witnessing Naomi's journey from emptiness to

fullness, through the actions of Ruth and Boaz. Her days of emptiness are soon to be over.

Naomi recognizes Boaz's serious commitment to meet with their
closer relative. She tells Ruth to wait "until you learn how the matter
turns out, for the man will not rest but will settle [accomplish, finish]
the matter today" (**3:18**). Naomi trusts Boaz to resolve the complication immediately, and so she urges Ruth to wait until he does just that.
Previously, she told Ruth to act; now she tells her to rest in the work
of Boaz. She believes Boaz to be a man of his word who will not leave
important work unfinished.

It is important to note that this is the last time we hear Ruth and
Naomi speak. They are present in chapter 4, but do not speak. Boaz
takes center stage, as the resolution to the crisis of the family line.
And behind it all is the hidden hand of God, accomplishing his sovereign purposes.

Our Redeemer

In the first part of Ruth 3, we saw Naomi make a plan which depend-
ed on the trustworthiness and integrity of Boaz. Next we saw Ruth go
beyond that plan with her bold proposal to Boaz. She not only trusted
him to do the right thing but showed her desire to pursue him and to
look after her mother-in-law. Given what we saw of Boaz in chapter
2, it does not surprise us that he responds with care and kindness. He
promises to help, and he sends Ruth away with a provision of grain
that hints at the future provision to come.

How similar this is to the way the Lord Jesus has dealt with us! We
can be like Ruth, going to him respectfully but boldly to ask him to
"spread [his] wings" over us and redeem us. He has made a promise
that all who call on his name will become part of his bride, the church
(Romans 10:9; Ephesians 5:28-33). And he has given us the most
wonderful provision: the Holy Spirit who dwells in us, the "firstfruits"
which promises more to come, assuring us of "the redemption of our
bodies" (Romans 8:23).

Ruth came to Boaz and asked him to be what she needed: a redeemer. Boaz not only promised marriage but also provided for her in the meantime. When we come to Christ, we too can ask for the redemption and provision that we are desperate for. Jesus has already seen us in our need, helpless at his feet, and has paid the price for us. He has spread his robes of righteousness over us and made us his own. He has given us the "good gifts"; supremely, the gift of the Holy Spirit (Luke 11:13). He has done all that we can ever ask him to do for us—and will continue to do all that we need him to.

Our Redeemer has changed everything. He has changed our status, brought us into intimate union with himself, and given us glorious hope for the future.

Questions for reflection

1. What are the similarities and differences between Boaz and Jesus in 3:6-18?

2. What would it look like for you to trust Jesus as Ruth trusted Boaz?

3. How could you become as trustworthy as Boaz?

7. THE CITY GATE

The Victorian preacher Charles Spurgeon famously said, "My entire theology can be condensed into four words: Jesus died for me." With humility and gratitude, all true Christians share this basic yet glorious confession.

However, as we grow in our faith, our understanding and appreciation of the meaning of Jesus' death should increase. New Christians have much to learn in the world of theology. They will attain a new vocabulary, learning words like **election**, atonement, **propitiation**, **expiation**, **satisfaction**, **justification**, **sanctification**, **glorification**, **eschatology**, and so on. But there is always a danger in learning theology, and it is this: losing sight of the personal nature of our faith. Hence the importance of the quote from Spurgeon. Jesus—a real person in human history, our Redeemer—died for me—a real person in desperate need.

As we learn theology we run the risk of loving a theological system more than Jesus. When we do so, we have lost sight of the very purpose of theology. We must never make the gospel mechanical, explaining our salvation as some kind of mathematical equation. Redemption, as we are seeing in the book of *Ruth*, is personal. This fact is one of the things that makes the book of *Ruth* so significant.

Not only must we keep the personal nature of salvation alive in our hearts, but we must also remember that we have been redeemed out of love. As we consider the theme of redemption, we find God acting on behalf of the weak and helpless out of his divine love. What should stir the affection of a true Christian is not the logical consistencies of a particular theological system—important though systematic theology is—but the wonder of Christ's love for sinners like us. It is the "romance" of this divine redemption, the intimacy of our union with Christ, "who loved [us] and gave himself for [us]" (Galatians 2:20), that inspires praise, adoration, and obedience. It is the beauty of a person, Jesus Christ, not the beauty of a theoretical system, that captivates our soul. Understanding the theology should only lead us to wonder more at the love and sacrifice of Jesus.

The storyline of love and redemption reaches back through the whole Bible. In Deuteronomy, Moses conveyed God's love in the work of redemption by saying, "He *loved* your fathers and chose their offspring after them and brought you out of Egypt with his own presence, by his great power" (Deuteronomy 4:37, my emphasis). This idea of redemption out of love is restated in chapter 7:

"The Lord your God has chosen you to be a people for his treasured possession, out of all the peoples who are on the face of the earth. It was not because you were more in number than any other people that the Lord set his *love* on you and chose you, for you were the fewest of all peoples, but it is because the Lord *loves* you and is keeping the oath that he swore to your fathers, that the Lord has brought you out with a mighty hand and *redeemed* you from the house of slavery, from the hand of Pharaoh king of Egypt." (Deuteronomy 7:6-8, my emphasis)

It was God's love for his child that motivated the exodus: "When Israel was a child, I loved him, and out of Egypt I called my son" (Hosea 11:1). In the New Testament we find the fullest expression of God's love motivating his redeeming work, expressed in various places and in various ways. Paul says that "God shows his love for us in that while we were still sinners, Christ died for us" (Romans 5:8). He tells the Ephesians, "Christ loved the church and gave himself up for her" (Ephesians 5:25). John begins the last book of the Bible by speaking of "him who loves us and has freed us from our sins by his blood and made us a kingdom, priests to his God and Father" (Revelation 1:5-6). The more we understand the theology while remembering that this redemption is personal—that Jesus died for *me*—the more we will be amazed by the love that motivated him. We must never get over or grow cold toward the holy romance of redemption.

Ruth gives us a concrete example of the Lord's personal and particular love for his bride. It is a little story within this larger story of redemption found along the storyline of the whole Bible. It helps us to keep sight of the personal, intimate, familial nature of redemption—of God's love for his beloved. And Ruth 4 brings this story of redemption to a close. The first half of the chapter (**4:1-12**) shows us Boaz seeking to resolve the matter of there being a closer relative who may choose to marry Ruth. These verses do not feature Ruth herself but show us the legal process by which Boaz redeems her. This may seem disappointing to anyone hoping for a romantic

> Redeeming Ruth is not straightforward. There is a price to pay. The question is: who will pay it?

wedding scene. But understanding the legal transaction discussed by Boaz and this other relative will help us to see how wonderful Boaz's redemption of Ruth is—just as understanding the theological depth of Christ's redemption should increase our appreciation of it. For redeeming Ruth is not straightforward: there is a price to pay. The question is: which man will pay it?

The Other Redeemer

The morning after the night before, Boaz goes up to the city gate and sits down (**4:1**). Legal transactions, judicial proceedings, and official business were all conducted at the city gate (Genesis 23:18; 34:20, 24; 2 Samuel 15:2–6; Proverbs 22:22; Amos 5:12, 15). It was a spacious place for people to assemble in, like a modern-day courthouse. Further, it was also the best place to find someone. Everyone in the city regularly passed through this gate. So Boaz sits here to wait for the other potential redeemer to come through.

"And behold, the redeemer, of whom Boaz had spoken, came by" (Ruth **4:1**). Again, the word "behold" is used to heighten the tension. We have already heard about this other possible redeemer (3:12), but now the meeting is about to take place!

Boaz greets this man, addressing him as his "friend," and asks him to sit with him. Once he is seated, Boaz asks the ruling body (ten of the town's **elders**) to sit down as well (**4:2**). It is unclear why the writer does not give us the name of this other man. Boaz would have known his name, and in court you need to know a person's name! Further, the book ends with a detailed genealogy, and so we may assume the writer knew Mr. So-and-so's name. His anonymity in the narrative may simply reflect the fact that he will be dismissed in the story and forgotten. But there could be more. Perhaps he is left anonymous to save his family from embarrassment; or the narrator might also be implying that this man is not worth naming, due to his self-centeredness and his failure to act on behalf of his relatives (**v 5-6**). Whatever the case, he sits down with Boaz to resolve this important matter before the elders at the gate.

The Right of Redemption

The necessary preparations made, Boaz explains the matter to the anonymous potential redeemer. We can imagine people gathered around the men and the elders, witnessing this interaction (see v 11). But **verse 3** does not begin in the way we would anticipate. Boaz does not begin with Ruth, but with Naomi and a piece of property belonging to Elimelech. It is this "parcel of land" that he tells the other redeemer he has the right to buy.

Raising this issue of Naomi's property first may be an intentional strategy of Boaz—he may be playing his cards carefully, diverting attention away from Ruth, in order to win Ruth for himself. Boaz responded with immediate positivity to Ruth's request (3:11), so it seems that he does indeed desire to marry her. Or, perhaps this is simply the most straightforward way of introducing the matter. After all, Boaz's gift to Naomi at the end of chapter 3 indicates that he was willing to do more than simply marry Ruth—his concern was for Naomi too. Perhaps this is why he now focuses on Naomi's property and her need to sell it.

Whichever, Boaz is doing nothing wrong or deceitful. After all, redeeming property was one of the customary roles of a *go'el* redeemer (Leviticus 25:25). By meeting the other relative at the city gate in the presence of the elders, Boaz is making sure that everything is above board. "I thought I would tell you of it," he says (Ruth **4:4**), acknowledging that although he himself wants to redeem the property, he must defer to the nearer relative first.

The land in question is all of Elimelech's property that had not been sold when the family made the journey to Moab (**v 9**). It was probably the only thing in Naomi's possession—all she had inherited from Elimelech. Presumably it was due to the desperate situation of herself and Ruth that Naomi needed to sell it. It would have been a crushing thing to have to do, especially given the fact that property was more significant to the Israelites than it is to us. God himself had divided up this land among the twelve tribes of Israel (Joshua 13 – 21). Those sections of land were then subdivided among clans and families. But the land was God's, not the people's. So land, spiritual life, and lineage were bound up together. No one would relocate outside the land for a job change or a career move. All of this explains why provision was made, in the laws about redeemers, for desperate Israelites who needed to sell their land (Leviticus 25:23-34). The nearest relative was to purchase it back from the buyer in order to keep it within the family. It was a law of love, not a means of financial gain, designed to prevent people taking advantage of the poverty of others.

In Ruth **4:4**, Boaz suggests using this law to buy the property. Having the first right of refusal, the other relative gets to decide whether he wants to acquire it first. If not, Boaz will commit to redeeming it. You can sense Boaz's eagerness to resolve things: "If you will not [redeem the property], tell me, that I may know, for there is no one besides you to redeem it, and I come after you."

The anonymous potential redeemer agrees to seize the opportunity before him, saying, "I will redeem it." He responds earnestly to the proposal. And why not? This was a good deal. Hubbard notes:

> "For very little money, he could carry out a respected family duty and perhaps enhance his civic reputation. Financially, the investment was a bargain without risk ... His little investment would develop into years of productive, profitable harvests; it would enlarge the inheritance of his heirs. How could he lose?"
>
> (*The Book of Ruth*, page 242)

But the deal is not yet final. He has only made his intentions known. And Boaz has something else to say.

Redeeming Ruth

Boaz next plays his ace—Ruth: "The day you buy the field from the hand of Naomi, you also acquire [that is, are required to marry] Ruth the Moabite, the widow of the dead, in order to perpetuate the name of the dead in his inheritance" (**v 5**).

There is a lot of discussion around the translation of this verse. Assuming the ESV's rendering (also reflected in many other modern English translations) is accurate, then Boaz is applying the spirit of the law to this situation, expecting the nearer relative to assume responsibility for both the property and Ruth. Thus, redeeming the property would involve more than personal gain. It would also involve sacrifice. To be sure, it would cost money to redeem the property; but redeeming Ruth by marriage as well would require resolve and even the risk of losing a good reputation (since, as Boaz emphasizes, Ruth is a Moabite).

Boaz also mentions "perpetuat[ing] the name of the dead in his inheritance." He is asking the other man to honor his family member's memory. In a culture such as this one, it was important not to let the name of a relative die out. This is why the law of levirate marriage existed (Deuteronomy 25:5), in order to raise a child for the dead man. In this specific case, the first son born in the new marriage would be recognized as the child of Mahlon—his mother Ruth's deceased first husband (Deuteronomy 25:6). This child would inherit the field when he grew up, perpetuating the name of the dead in the inherited land.

Upon further review, the unnamed kinsman balks at the proposal, saying, "I cannot redeem it for myself, lest I impair my own inheritance. Take my right of redemption yourself, for I cannot redeem it" (Ruth **4:6**). The sacrifice was too great for him. Duguid explains why the deal just became far less attractive to him:

> "If there were to be a child from the relationship with Ruth, the redeemer would lose the field and there would be no benefit to his own children and estate to compensate for the costs involved in taking care of Naomi and Ruth. In other words, Mr. So-and-So was interested in ministry to the poor only if there was a payoff for himself and his family." (*Esther & Ruth*, page 182)

The narrator does not explain all the details of the laws here. The point is that we notice the interests and attitudes of the two potential redeemers. The anonymous relative's interest is in himself. He is more concerned with his own welfare, property, and posterity than with the welfare of his relative, Naomi. So he urges Boaz to redeem her property and her daughter-in-law.

A true redeemer is the kind of person who is willing to pay a price for the good of others, and that is a mark of Boaz, not the other relative. It is fitting that no one knows this man's name, while Boaz, who reflects the selfless love of Christ (Philippians 2:1-11), is remembered as a member of the line of the Messiah.

Questions for reflection

1. "Understanding the theology should only lead us to wonder more at the love and sacrifice of Jesus." How can you make sure this is true of you? How can you help others to wonder more at Jesus?

2. In your experience, what reasons do people have for helping the poor?

3. What price might the Lord be calling you to pay for the good of others?

PART TWO

Sealing the Deal

That matter is now settled. Boaz is willing to pay the price necessary to marry Ruth, and the closer relative is not—and so Boaz's "purchase" is confirmed through an ancient custom: "When the redeemer said to Boaz, 'Buy it for yourself,' he drew off his sandal" (Ruth **4:8**).

The phrase "custom in former times" (**v 7**) tells us that the writer is writing after this particular time period; he is explaining a practice that is no longer in use in his own times. He is describing a form of "hand-shake" which confirmed the deal—the removal of a sandal was prob-ably associated with walking the land as a symbol of ownership (see Joshua 1:3). "Feet" often symbolized power, possession, and domina-tion (see in particular Isaiah 66:1 and Matthew 22:44; and also Psalm 110:1 and 1 Samuel 25:23-24). Boaz had possession of both Ruth and the property (contrast this event with the different but similar custom in Deuteronomy 25:7-10). Regardless of the origins of the practice, the point is that the deal has now been confirmed.

With the official business complete, Boaz offers a speech; he states that he has bought the field from Naomi and redeemed Ruth to be his wife (Ruth **4:9-10**). He bookends his speech with the phrase "You are witnesses," just in case any future questions arise concerning the transaction. The first part of the speech focuses on the estate of Elimelech (**v 9**), while the second part focuses on the person of Ruth (**v 10**). We can recognize the role of a *go'el* from Deuteronomy 25: he is marrying Ruth "to perpetuate the name of the dead in his in-heritance, that the name of the dead may not be cut off from among his brothers and from the gate of his native place" (Ruth **4:10**). Boaz also reiterates the phrase "this day," which again highlights his zeal to fulfill his promise to Ruth (3:13, 18). The redeemer has resolved the matter, as he said he would.

A Three-fold Blessing

Now the meeting is over. The negotiations are finished. The legal process is done. Boaz has given his speech. But one more significant thing happens at the city gate: a three-fold prayer of blessing from the people and the elders.

The first blessing is directed to Ruth: "May the LORD make the woman, who is coming into your house, like Rachel and Leah, who together built up the house of Israel" (**4:11a**). Rachel and Leah were the wives of Jacob: with their two handmaidens (or "servants," ESV), Bilhah and Zilpah, they bore him twelve sons, whose descendants made up the twelve tribes of Israel (Genesis 29 – 30; 35:16-18—again, remember that narrative is descriptive, not prescriptive). The Lord is the One who enabled both Leah and Rachel to have children; in each case he "opened her womb" (29:31; 30:22). Leah was the mother of Judah (29:35), the ancestor of the tribe of Naomi and Boaz. The people, then, are asking the Lord to give Ruth a place alongside these mothers of the people of God: that is, that she may be given a key role among God's people.

The second prayer of blessing is pointed toward Boaz: "May you act worthily in **Ephrathah** and be renowned in Bethlehem" (Ruth **4:11b**). This is not just a prayer for prosperity and a good reputation; it is a prayer for righteousness. Boaz's renown will come from his worthy actions—the kindness, compassion, and integrity that we have seen in the book of *Ruth*.

The final blessing is directed to the family as a whole: "And may your house be like the house of Perez, whom Tamar bore to Judah" (**v 12**). Tamar was the widow of Judah's son (Genesis 38:6-7). She too had lost her husband and was childless. As with Ruth, Tamar's family line was threatened, and it seemed that her husband's name would die out. Tamar had no prospect of marrying again: her father-in-law, Judah, had promised that she would marry another of his sons, as the law demanded, but he had not kept his promise (v 11, 14). So Tamar disguised herself as a prostitute, deceiving her own father-in-law, so that she might have a child by him (v 15-16).

Both Ruth and Tamar went out in active pursuit of a child and a better future. Of course, Ruth revealed her identity and received a child legitimately through marriage, whereas Tamar concealed her identity and deceived Judah. Moreover, Boaz's behavior toward Ruth was only ever godly, whereas Judah's conduct was precisely the opposite. Both unions, however, in the providence of God, proved to play an important role in salvation history. God promised that the Messiah would come through Judah (Genesis 49:10), and Judah's strongest son was Perez; of all the sons of Judah, it is Perez's descendants whose line is followed in the tribal genealogy of 1 Chronicles 2:3 – 3:24.

The women's third prayer is for Boaz to have a renowned lineage in Bethlehem. Little did they know just how great Bethlehem would be because of his descendants! David, Israel's greatest king, would come from Boaz's family in Bethlehem—and, of course, eventually the Messiah would come from the same family tree (Matthew 1:1-17).

So these prayers were answered. Ruth did become a key person in the story of redemptive history. Boaz's family did have renown in Bethlehem. And it was through Boaz that Israel's king would come. At this point, the people of Israel had not even asked for a king (though they did need one—Judges 21:25), but from this man, Boaz, King David would emerge.

The last phrase, "because of the offspring that the LORD will give you by this young woman" (Ruth **4:12**), is significant: it points to how Ruth and Boaz's future would contain such blessings, and ultimately to how sinners would be redeemed. The word translated "offspring" also means "seed"—an important subject in redemptive history. The references to Leah, Rachel, and Tamar and the reference to "seed" would have made the audience think of certain significant promises in the Old Testament which are linked to offspring and descendants. In the third chapter of Genesis, for example, we read of what some call the "first gospel." God says to his enemy, the serpent, "I will put enmity between you and the woman, and between your offspring and her offspring; he shall bruise your head, and you shall bruise his heel" (Genesis 3:15). From this point onward, readers are waiting on this promised one who would crush the head of the serpent, Satan. Likewise, God promised Abraham offspring and said that he would establish a covenant with those descendants (17:4-8). Eventually, our Redeemer came through an even more extraordinary birth than the childbearing of Ruth and the barren matriarchs of Israel (Matthew 1:18-25). Through the virgin Mary, in the fullness of time, Christ our Savior was born to redeem a people for himself (Galatians 4:4-7).

The Ultimate Love Story

The narrator does not tell us how the news got back to Ruth and Naomi. We can imagine the various possibilities. Were Ruth and Naomi watching for Boaz's arrival? Did he hide the sandal behind his back, whip it out, and say, *Surprise! You are now my bride!*? We do not know. All we are told next is that Boaz took Ruth as his wife (Ruth **4:13**).

One thing is for certain: Boaz was unique. To be a redeemer, one needed to be a relative and to have the willingness to redeem. The nearer relative was not willing to pay the price, but Boaz was. He was "a mighty good man."

There is much to learn from this love story—though the story of Ruth and Boaz is not exactly like modern-day love stories. While it does display two unlikely people uniting (a popular theme in modern love stories), it highlights, instead of good looks or passionate feelings, the good character of the two individuals. What made Boaz and Ruth such a perfect match? They were both individuals of "worthy" character (2:1; 3:11) whom the Lord brought together. Again Proverbs 31 is instructive. The mother of the king (v 1) tells her son not to be distracted by instant pleasure but to look for a wife who has many of the same characteristics that we find in Ruth—strength, dignity, wisdom, and kindness (Proverbs 31:25-26).

Always remember—whether you are unmarried or seeking to counsel friends who are (and we should all be one or other of those)—the importance of godliness in a potential spouse. Ruth is a model bride: the kind of woman that Christian men should long to marry. She is a true convert; she shows kindness; she works hard; she is humble; she has a gutsy faith; she is pure; and she is patient. In short, she is like Jesus. Boaz is a model groom: the kind of man that Christian women should long to marry. He is a man of moral character; he prays; he protects; he provides; he serves; he works; he integrates his faith and work; he is pure; he obeys Scripture; and he is selfless. In short, he too is like Jesus.

Most importantly, Boaz was willing to pay the price. The reluctance of the other relative to marry Ruth and his concern about his own inheritance highlight the amazing commitment and selflessness of Boaz, who laid down his own interests to redeem Ruth. The narrator shows us the legal implications of redemption in order that we may see the love that motivates it.

The same is true for the greater love story surrounding the story of Ruth and Boaz—the epic love story of Jesus the Redeemer and the people he has redeemed. Boaz was special, but our Redeemer, Jesus Christ, is even more special. Boaz may have impaired his inheritance to redeem Ruth, but Jesus was actually willing to empty himself and go to the cross to secure our redemption. In his great love, he laid down his life for his bride. He redeemed us because he loved us (Ephesians 5:25). The story of *Ruth* gives us a concrete example of the romance of redemption and points us to this even greater union, of which every Christian, single or married, is a part and a beneficiary.

We must never lose the wonder of our Redeemer's love for us, displayed most fully at the cross. Duguid reflects on this love:

"There, in the midst of darkness far deeper than any ordinary midnight, he offered himself up for the sins of the people. There he was abandoned by God the Father, who turned aside his face because he would not and could not look upon his own Son, disfigured as he was bearing our sin. Jesus did not risk his life; he gave it. Why? Is it because we are such wonderful people and we thoroughly deserve it? Certainly not! It is because God was so committed to saving sinners like us, and this was the only way it could be done. It is because God loved the world so much that he gave his one and only Son, that whoever believes in him should not perish but have everlasting life (see John 3:16)."

(Esther & Ruth, page 177-178)

We should pause and ask ourselves: *do I know this love? Have I entered into the most important of all relationships? Is my appreciation of the character and love of my Redeemer growing?*

If we do know this love, then we cannot keep it to ourselves. The book of *Ruth* is shouting to us not only about God's heart for us but also about God's heart for the nations. He takes outsiders and makes them insiders, as they hear and respond to the good news. As we consider the plight of the nations today, and the oppression found in false religions, will we ask the Lord to give us an opportunity to tell someone about the greatest of all love stories? Do not be surprised at what the Lord may do. He answered the prayers at the city gate in Ruth 4. And he has been known to convert the most unlikely of people, and even use them as significant figures in the drama of redemption! Let us keep this prayer in our hearts—for the Lord to use us to make his good news known. May words from another hymn of William Cowper's be true of us: "Redeeming love has been my theme, and shall be till I die."

Questions for reflection

1. When you talk to unmarried friends about seeking a spouse, how could the book of Ruth inform what you say?

2. How does the story of Ruth grow your appreciation of the character and love of your Redeemer? What difference will that make to you this week?

3. Who could you share the truth of Jesus' redeeming love with this week?

8. THE SON

Recently my wife, Kimberly, and I went on a double date with some friends. After dinner, we decided to go axe throwing. This is a popular activity now (at least in North Carolina!). It is the new bowling. We had never been axe throwing—we do not even like camping! But to our surprise, Kimberly excelled at it. She won nine straight matches against different guys in the arena. She was so good that workers came out from behind the cash register to watch her throw. They also begged her to join the league! I left our date wondering if I should be encouraged by her feat or warned by it; I have never watched *So I Married an Axe Murderer,* but maybe I should! We are celebrating our fifteenth year of marriage this month, and it is amazing how I continue to learn things about my spouse as the years go on. I never thought Kimberly would be an all-star axe thrower. She continues to captivate me.

The book of *Ruth* is about a marriage between two captivating people. As each chapter unfolds, we continue to learn things from Ruth and Boaz, and things about Ruth and Boaz. The most important of those have revolved around the character of these two people— these "worthy" individuals (2:1; 3:11).

However, we have also kept in mind that *Ruth* is set within the greater love story of Scripture, the epic story of redemption. Behind the scenes, working out his providential plan to bring King David to his throne, and eventually his own Son, King Jesus, to his, is the Almighty. As heroic as Ruth, Boaz, and David may be, they are always secondary to the ultimate Hero. The more we get to know the Bible, the more we will get to know the Lord. We finish the book of *Ruth* captivated, recognizing that God alone deserves the glory for his work in redemptive history.

God Has Not Forgotten His People

In this closing section of *Ruth*, the narrator ties up some of the dominant ideas in the book, showing how God has not forgotten Naomi and Ruth, nor, by extension, the people of God. Those who so desperately need a king will be provided with one. First there is a summary showing how God filled Naomi's emptiness with satisfaction (**4:13-17**), and then there is a genealogy pointing to God's ongoing work through this family (v 18-21). It is tempting to read genealogies quickly without pondering their significance, but this genealogy is vital to understanding what is taking place in *Ruth*: a bigger story is being told. This genealogy is later reflected in Matthew's genealogy of Jesus. After we examine the conclusion of *Ruth*, we will also consider the introduction to Matthew's Gospel, in order to see more fully the staggering providence of God and the glory of Jesus our Redeemer.

The narrator shows us four ways God was at work in the lives of Naomi, Ruth, and Boaz, accomplishing his far-reaching purposes through them: God provides a son for Boaz and Ruth, a redeemer for Naomi, a king for Israel, and the Messiah for the world.

God Provides a Son for Boaz and Ruth

"So Boaz took Ruth, and she became his wife. And he went in to her, and the LORD gave her conception, and she bore a son" (**v 13**). From wedding to baby in one verse! Saying that Boaz "took Ruth" is to say that "he took her home," an expression for marriage (see v 11). Then the narrator says, "and she became his wife." This seems redundant—it is saying the same thing a second time—but its inclusion emphasizes Ruth's new status. It is encouraging to look back at Ruth's story and see how far she has come. She has been repeatedly called "the Moabite." She called herself the "foreigner" (2:10). She identified herself as being lower than a servant (2:13). She then elevated herself to the level of "servant" when proposing to Boaz (3:9). But here in chapter 4, she is Ruth, the wife of Boaz. She has a brand new status, thanks to the sovereign grace of God.

Not only this, but God gives her a child. Boaz, we are told, "went in to her" (**4:13**). That is, he entered the bridal chamber in order to sleep with her. But the more important phrase is "the LORD gave her conception."

The two great needs in the book of *Ruth* are fertility and food. The fertility of the land has been an issue all the way through the story, from the famine that drove Naomi and her family to Moab (1:1) to the harvest that Ruth and Boaz took part in (chapter 2), to the grain that Boaz sent with Ruth as a gift to Naomi (3:17). The very first verses of the book also emphasized the childlessness of Naomi's sons (1:5). The role of the redeemer was also connected with fertility, as the redeemer of a widow was to raise a son on behalf of his relative (4:10)—Ruth needed a son in order to honor her dead husband.

How have those needs been met? By the Lord's intervention. Only two times does the narrator explicitly mention the Lord's involvement in this story: once regarding his provision of food (1:6) and now with his provision of a son (**4:13**). In both cases, the message is clear: God has not forgotten his servants. He is the One who provides for their needs.

The Lord's involvement in the birth of this child is not just an important statement for the love story of Boaz and Ruth; it is also part of an important thread in the grand story of the Bible. Throughout the biblical narrative, God intervenes in order to bring forth children who are significant in redemptive history. Often these children are born of women who were previously childless—something which highlights the fact that it is the Lord who enables these births. In Genesis 21, Sarah cannot conceive until the Lord intervenes (Genesis 21:1). As a result, Isaac is born even when she is past the menopause (18:10-21; 21:2-3). In Genesis 25, Isaac's wife, Rebekah, is also unable to have children, but the Lord answers Isaac's prayer and she conceives, giving birth to Jacob and Esau (25:21-26). In Genesis 29 – 30, God enables both Leah and barren Rachel, the mothers of the people of God, to conceive. Later in the Bible, Hannah is barren, but the Lord grants her the ability to have a son: Samuel, who will herald the coming of King David (1 Samuel 1:19-20). In each case, God is saying, *Keep your eye on this child! He will play a vital role in accomplishing my purposes.*

In *Ruth*, the narrator wants us to know that Ruth belongs to this significant group of mothers, just as the women at the city gate prayed (Ruth 4:11). In Moab, during ten years of marriage, she did not have children, but now the Lord enables her to have a son. Ruth carried her child to full term until "she bore a son." We are left to wonder, "What role will this child play in the advancement of God's purposes?"

God Provides a Redeemer for Naomi

Naomi has gone from emptiness to fullness. The women around Naomi recognize this transformation. When Naomi first entered town, the women asked, "Is this Naomi?" Naomi responded to the buzz in town by insisting that she be called "Mara" ("bitter") instead of Naomi ("sweet"). But now, a great reversal has taken place. The women of Bethlehem recognize this: their congratulations for the birth of the child go not to Ruth, but to Naomi.

The women first praise God: "Blessed be the LORD, who has not left you this day without a redeemer, and may his name be renowned in Israel!" (**v 14**). God alone deserves the glory for this reversal. Naomi once said that "the hand of the LORD has gone out against me" (1:13), but in fact God's hand was with Naomi. He gave her a child.

This child is also called "a redeemer" (**4:14**). Surprisingly, this word does not refer to Boaz but to his son. Ruth's son will bless Naomi personally, and will continue the family line. This child, in other words, will save the day.

Next, the women convey a heartfelt wish for the child to be "renowned in Israel." That may seem like just a nice sentiment—and we know children do not always live up to our expectations and desires. However, in this case, the child will indeed become famous in Israel!

The genealogy in the following verses tells us that through this child, Obed, Old Testament Israel's greatest king would come.

The women then express to Naomi their confidence about what Ruth's son will be like: "He shall be to you a restorer of life and a nourisher of your old age, for your daughter-in-law who loves you, who is more to you than seven sons, has given birth to him" (**v 15**). The child will restore her life, by giving her renewed vitality and joy. He will renew Naomi's heart by continuing the family line. He will also "nourish" her in old age by providing the basic necessities of life. Remember that the two basic needs at the end of chapter 1 were food and children. This child will solve both problems. This is what makes him a redeemer.

The final part of the women's expressed confidence is related to Ruth. How can we be sure that this child will restore and nourish Naomi? The women point to his mother. They are guaranteeing the child's future care of Naomi on the basis of Ruth's character—on Ruth's love for Naomi. Ruth's devotion to Naomi is so great that having her is better than having seven sons. Seven was a number of perfection and sons were highly prized; and it was the loss of her sons that was a key reason for Naomi's bitterness in chapter 1. This expression is the ultimate tribute to Ruth's amazing life and loyalty.

The result is that this child will not merely serve a legal function as the heir of Elimelech. Ruth has in a sense given him to Naomi. This relationship between Naomi and Obed will be more than a typical grandmother-grandson relationship. The child will be concerned for the wellbeing of Naomi. This is because of God's *hesed*, his kindness, worked through the *hesed* of Ruth, who has displayed remarkable devotion to Naomi from the beginning to the end of this narrative.

Naomi's journey from emptiness to fullness is illustrated in the next sentence: "Then Naomi took the child and laid him on her lap and became his nurse" (**v 16**). She had been empty, having no food and no child. Now her arms are full—holding this little boy. The word "nurse" paints her as a nanny or guardian: again, a mark of the special relationship the two will have. Some even suggest that this is an adoption ritual, but I think that is reading too much into the text. Block notes:

> "Within this family context these are not legal actions but the loving, natural actions of a grandmother, gratefully accepting her new status and tenderly receiving the baby. Within the context of the book, however, the action is much more significant. The image of this woman taking the child in her arms must also be seen against the backdrop of her previous experience. She had not only had her bread basket emptied by famine; in the deaths of her husband and sons her bosom had also been emptied of her men." (*Judges, Ruth*, page 730)

God had not forgotten Naomi. The boy in her bosom, a little redeemer, proved it. She had gone from emptiness to fullness, from bitterness to happiness.

God Provides a King for Israel

"And the women of the neighborhood gave him a name, saying, 'A son has been born to Naomi.' They named him Obed. He was the father of Jesse, the father of David" (**v 17**). The mention of David alerts us to the fact that Obed was not the end of the story. The narrator reveals a surprise—there is more! To Ruth, a childless widow, God had provided a husband and a son. To Naomi—an older, bitter widow whose family line was close to extinction—God had provided Obed. Next, to a nation close to extinction, God provided a king.

> To a widow, God provided a son. To a nation close to extinction, God provided a king.

The book of *Ruth* is not just a story about two desperate widows—it is a story about a desperate nation on the verge of annihilation. Remember the last verse in Judges: "There was no king in Israel" (Judges 21:25). It was a broken nation whose immorality and disunity threatened its survival (Judges 21:16-18). Remember the first person mentioned in *Ruth*: Elimelech, which means "My God is King" (Ruth 1:2). But Elimelech did not live up to his name, and he certainly did not lead Israel out of darkness—far from it. He fled to Moab and died. Obed, however—his grandson by levirate marriage— would be the grandfather of David, the king who would solve Israel's problem by giving God's people leadership, unity, and security. And Obed would also be the ancestor of the King who would solve the world's problem by bringing perfect leadership and complete forgiveness and eternal life.

One more important note about **4:17**: it was the women who named Obed. This does not mean that Ruth and Boaz had no influence on the name of Obed; but this chorus of voices indicates something special. This child would be of great significance. The name "Obed" is short for Obadiah, which means "servant of Yahweh"—a description that many men in the Old Testament possessed (see, for instance, 1 Kings 18:1-16; 1 Chronicles 3:21; 7:3; 9:16; Ezra 8:9). Obed would serve Naomi directly, but he would also serve the nation of Israel, as from his line came the ultimate servant (Isaiah 52:13 – 53:12; Mark 10:45).

Questions for reflection

1. What has captivated you in the book of Ruth?

2. How have you seen God's provision throughout the story?

3. Look at the women's praise in verses 14-15. What could you praise God for in a similar way?

PART TWO

God Provides the Messiah for the World

History is not a series of wretched events, one thing after another, going nowhere. The story of *Ruth* is so important because it reminds us that history is moving to the worship of Jesus Christ, who is the "root and the descendant of David" (Revelation 22:16).

Ruth concludes with that short genealogy listing the line of Boaz—both his ancestors and his descendants:

> "Now these are the generations of Perez: Perez fathered Hezron, Hezron fathered Ram, Ram fathered Amminadab, Amminadab fathered Nahshon, Nahshon fathered Salmon, Salmon fathered Boaz, Boaz fathered Obed, Obed fathered Jesse, and Jesse fathered David." (Ruth **4:18-22**)

These ten names display God's answer to the prayer that Boaz may be renowned in Bethlehem and that his house may be like that of Perez (v 11-12). The name "Perez" recalls that prayer. Perez heads the royal line of Judah, which continues through a host of others to Boaz, Obed, Jesse, and finally David. The list is not exhaustive—there would have been other members of the family in between the names we read here (see 1 Chronicles 2). But it is meant to show the continuation of the line. Hubbard suggests that the author tailors this genealogy to fit a ten-member scheme because that was the traditional way to present a royal genealogy (*The Book of Ruth*, pages 280-281).

David, the offspring of Jesse, was Israel's most celebrated king. Not only was he a military hero who defeated the Philistines, and not only did he capture Jerusalem, where God's temple would be built (2 Samuel 5); but the prophets declared him to be the **paradigm** for the future Messiah (Ezekiel 37:24-25; Matthew 22:42). Further, God promised that one of King David's sons would sit on the throne forever (2 Samuel 7:12b-16; Psalm 132:12). All of this comes to fulfillment in Jesus. He is the greater David. The people in Jerusalem declared to

Jesus, "Hosanna to the Son of David!" (Matthew 21:9). Paul opens the book of Romans by saying that Jesus "was descended from David according to the flesh" (Romans 1:3; see also Acts 13:22-23).

Indeed, this genealogy has an even greater significance than showing us how the story of *Ruth* solves Israel's need for a king. It also appears somewhere else in the Scriptures, in Matthew 1. Matthew's genealogy does not end with David but with David's greater son, Jesus. The genealogy in *Ruth*, it turns out, is a part of the larger royal line leading up to the Servant King, Jesus.

The first sentence of Matthew's genealogy (Matthew 1:1) gives us the highlights. Notice the first person mentioned: David. Jesus is the descendant of King David—the "Christ," which means the Anointed One, the Messiah (it is not his last name!). Jesus is the honored son of David who would sit on the throne, as promised (see Isaiah 9:6-7; 11:1-10; Jeremiah 23:5-6). Next, Abraham is mentioned—the one through whom God promised to bless the nations (Genesis 12:1-3; 15:1-6). These two giants in redemptive history point to the nature of Jesus, the promised King, who would bless the nations. And this Jesus appeared in human history.

The Messiah Saves Sinners

Why did Matthew decide to begin his book with a genealogy? First, he was writing to a primarily Jewish audience who had placed their trust in Jesus as the long-awaited Messiah or who were considering believing in Jesus as the Messiah. This genealogy showed them that Jesus was not something new but had always been part of God's plans.

Second, Matthew's genealogy says something theological: Jesus Christ came into the world to save sinners (1 Timothy 1:15). This is evident in the story of his birth in Matthew 1:18-25. An angel of the Lord appears to Joseph, explains that Mary is pregnant, and instructs him to "call [the child's] name Jesus, for he will save his people from their sins" (v 21). "Jesus" (v 1, 21, 25) is Greek for "Joshua" or "Yeshua," meaning "God saves." His name matches the angel's description: "He will save his people from their sins" (v 21).

The genealogy, too, makes it clear that God has always saved broken sinners, incorporated them into his people, and used them to further his plans. This is shown by the surprising fact that Ruth and some other key women appear. Women were not usually included in the genealogies, since descent was traced through the men. But here five interesting women are included.

The first woman Matthew lists is Tamar (v 3), the mother of Perez and Zerah, who had deceived and slept with her own father-in-law, Judah (Genesis 38). Then Matthew mentions Rahab (Matthew 1:5). She was a prostitute in Jericho who saved two Israelite spies and became part of God's people (Joshua 2:1-21; 6:25); most notably for our study of Ruth, she was the mother of Boaz (which perhaps goes some way to explaining why Boaz was so quick to notice and welcome Ruth, another woman who had grown up among Israel's enemies but had now come to settle among Israel). Third, Matthew notes Ruth herself, the Moabite.

In the second set of fourteen names, in which Israel's kings up to the exile are listed (Matthew 1:7-11), Matthew mentions Bathsheba, calling her "the wife of Uriah" (v 6). This reminds us that Bathsheba, the mother of David's son King Solomon, was brought into the family line through adultery and murder (2 Samuel 11). Finally, the concluding set of 14 generations goes from the deportation to Babylon to the birth of Jesus Christ (Matthew 1:12-16). There we find the fifth woman to be mentioned: Mary (v 16).

It is unexpected enough to mention women in a genealogy of this time, but when we consider the stories of these particular women, we may be even more surprised. This genealogy demonstrates the fact that God redeems and works his purposes out through sinners. Judah and David were both mighty and significant men, but it is their extramarital unions with Tamar and Bathsheba respectively that are mentioned, and this serves to highlight their sin. The stories of both

Rahab and Ruth, meanwhile, show us how the unlikeliest outsiders—a prostitute in Jericho and a widow from Moab—can end up playing a significant role in the plans of God.

As we read the story of the inclusion of Ruth into the family of Boaz—which is also the family of Judah, Tamar, Perez, and Rahab—and hear the genealogy of her descendants leading up to David, we should remember that she is only one example of a pattern that runs throughout the history of God's people, and that culminates with Jesus: the saving of sinners.

This genealogy includes prostitutes, adulterers, liars, and murderers. It includes both men and women, both Jews and non-Jews. None are disqualified from being used by God. Here they are in the genealogy of Jesus, his Son, our Messiah!

The Messiah Brings Peace

In the book of *Ruth*, we have read about the need for "refuge" and "rest." We have seen how Ruth took refuge "under the wings" of Israel's God and ended up with a "worthy" husband and a child. We have read about Naomi's struggle: how she thought God was against her and how, at the end of the story, she found out that God had not forgotten her. But think of the way in which they received this provision from the Lord. Were they handed some money and left on their own? No! Naomi experiences the extraordinary devotion of Ruth. Both women experience the extraordinary kindness of Boaz. The story ends with the picture of Naomi holding a child in her arms. The redemption is not a mere legal process. Ruth and Naomi find real rest, peace, and intimacy.

The same is true, in an even more glorious way, for Christians today. After the genealogy, Matthew 1 tells us the story of how an even more significant son is born in Bethlehem with an even more remarkable birth. Obed was a "redeemer," "a restorer of life and a nourisher of ... old age" (Ruth 4:14-15); but Jesus is even better. Matthew 1:23 tells us that Jesus would be called "Immanuel," which means "God with us." Not only has God not forgotten us, but God is with us. By placing our faith in Jesus Christ, we find ultimate refuge, ultimate rest, and ultimate peace. He has come to give rest to the weak and weary, the sick and sore. It is reported that the great eighteenth-century **evangelist** and preacher John Wesley said on his deathbed, "The best of all, God is with us. Farewell." But this is not just a truth to die with—it is a truth to live with.

The book of Matthew begins with this assurance of God's presence with us, and it closes with Jesus' promise, "I am with you always" (Matthew 28:20). This is an "already" promise for all who trust in Jesus as Messiah. Right now, through the Holy Spirit, we can experience God's presence in a powerful and intimate way. But it is also a "not yet" promise. One day, this promise will come to its climactic fulfillment. In the new heavens and new earth, John tells us that God will "dwell with them." We "will be his people" and "God himself will be with [us]" as our God (Revelation 21:3). He will wipe all the tears from our eyes, and he will make all things new (v 5). All this is conveyed by the name "Immanuel."

And how would this Jesus come to be with us, providing this grace, peace, and joy for sinners? Matthew tells us that a "virgin" would conceive (Matthew 1:23). He reiterates this point two verses later: "[Joseph] knew her not [that is, he did not sleep with her] until she had given birth to a son" (v 25). Here is yet another remarkable birth, bringing forth a significant son.

Luke tells us that prior to Jesus' birth, Mary's relative Elizabeth had been barren (Luke 1:7). But the Lord sent an angel to tell her husband, Zechariah, that Elizabeth would bear a son, by the Lord's intervention. Her son, John the Baptist, would prepare the way for the Messiah. And all these noteworthy, unusual conceptions in redemptive history (those of Sarah, Rebekah, Rachel, Hannah, and Elizabeth) prepare us for the most significant of all: the conception of Jesus. This time God's intervention was even more impressive: the previous mothers struggled to conceive, but Mary was a virgin. Jesus' arrival was the most extraordinary conception and birth of all time.

We might say that in Matthew 1 the genealogy shows us the human nature of Jesus, but the story of the virgin birth magnifies his divine nature. Jesus Christ is fully God and fully man, united in one person. This is the mystery of the incarnation, the glory of Christmas (see Galatians 4:4-7). This is "God with us." Jesus did not decree salvation from afar. He came to help us, to deal kindly with us, to die for us, to remain with us by his Spirit, and one day to bring us to be with himself forever.

This is the ultimate significance of the book of *Ruth*. It began with a family who had turned away from God's people and a woman who was full of bitterness. It tells us the story of two worthy individuals, Ruth and Boaz, who sought to serve the Lord and, as a result, brought a resolution to Naomi's crisis. It ends with David, God's chosen king. But all the way through, it points to Jesus Christ. He is unique: the only person in the God-man category. He is the only one qualified to fully redeem us, to save us from our sins, to make us his beloved, and to give us a glorious inheritance. And he loves us so much that he gave up everything he had in order to do all this.

> Because of Jesus, there is no need for bitterness over our circumstances and no reason to compromise in our obedience.

For Christians, therefore, there is an even greater resolution than the one experienced by Naomi in *Ruth*. For us, there is no need for bitterness over our circumstances and no reason to compromise in our obedience. We live in the light of the glorious birth of Jesus. We rejoice in the saving grace of Jesus. We rest in the already-but-not-yet peace of Jesus, Ruth and Boaz's descendant and the church's great Redeemer:

The bride eyes not her garment,
But her dear bridegroom's face;
I will not gaze at glory
But on my King of grace;
Not at the crown he giveth
But on his pierced hand:
The Lamb is all the glory
Of Immanuel's land. (Anne Ross Cousin)

Questions for reflection

1. Consider the characters in the story: Ruth, Naomi, Boaz, Obed, and the women in Bethlehem. In what ways does each one point to Christ or to followers of Christ?

2. How could Matthew's genealogy help you when talking to someone who thinks they are not good enough to be a Christian?

3. How does the story of Ruth give you confidence in Jesus?

GLOSSARY

Abba: Hebrew word for "Father" which Jesus used to address God the Father.

Alphabetic acrostic: a poem in which each line begins with the next letter of the alphabet

Atoning: providing a way of coming back into relationship with someone.

Bar mitzvah: a Jewish coming-of-age ritual.

Canaanite nations: the people of Canaan and related nations who lived among or around the nation of Israel. Canaanites did not worship the God of Israel.

Canonical order: the order in which the books of the Bible are traditionally placed.

Chiastic: a structure in which ideas or words are nested within one another. The first and the last statements match, as do the second and second-last, and so on.

Commentators: people who write books studying (or, more broadly, who offer opinions regarding) biblical texts.

Confession: a statement of what somebody believes.

Covenant faithfulness: God's commitment to uphold the binding agreement he made with Abraham and his descendants (i.e. the nation of Israel).

Creed: a formal statement of Christian belief (e.g. the **Apostles' Creed**, the **Nicene Creed**).

Doctrine: the study of what is true about God; or a statement about an aspect of that truth.

Elders: a group of men who are responsible for leadership.

Election: the idea that God chooses people to follow him.

Elijah, Elisha: two Old Testament prophets (see 1 Kings 17 – 22; 2 Kings 1 – 13).

Ephrathah: another name for Bethlehem.

Eschatology: the study of the end times, including death, judgment, and the new creation.

Evangelist: someone who shares the good news about Jesus.

Exodus: literally "way out" or "departure"; the historical period when the people of Israel left slavery in Egypt and began to travel toward the promised land.

Expiation: the act of making amends for something you have done wrong. Jesus expiates or makes amends for our sin.

Expositional: a detailed explanation of a Bible passage.

Fallen: affected by God's judgment that was a consequence of the fall—the event when the first man and woman disobeyed God (Genesis 3).

Fatalism: thinking that what will happen will happen and so there is no point doing anything to try to change it.

Gentiles: people who are not ethnically Jewish.

Gideon: a judge or leader of God's people (see Judges 6 – 8).

Glorification: the moment when one of God's people is made perfect, like Christ, and welcomed into God's eternal kingdom.

Gospel: the proclamation that the man Jesus was also God himself, who has come to serve us and to rule us as our King; that he died for sins; that he rose to rule and give new life; that he is reigning in heaven and will return to restore the world. The gospel is good news to be believed, not good advice to be followed.

Heresy: a belief which directly opposes the biblical gospel.

Horn: a symbol in the Bible of strength and honor.

Incarnation: the coming of the divine Son of God as a human, in the person of Jesus Christ.

Indentured service: a type of service in between employment and slavery. This type of servant worked without pay (often in order to work off a debt) but was not permanently enslaved.

Jacob: the son of Isaac, grandson of Abraham, and brother of Esau (see Genesis 25 – 50).

Job: the main character of the book of Job, a righteous man who is tested by Satan.

Joseph: the second-youngest son of Jacob (see Genesis 30:22-24; 37 – 50).

Jubilee: a year of celebration, resting and restoration which God told the Israelites to observe every fiftieth year (after seven cycles of seven years).

Judah: the third-oldest son of Jacob (see Genesis 29:35; 37; 42 – 50), who gave his name to the tribe of Judah and the land they inhabited, which included the city of Jerusalem. Later Judah became a separate kingdom from the rest of Israel.

Justification: the declaration that somebody is not guilty.

Kosher: allowed according to Old Testament law. This originally referred to food which Jews were allowed to eat.

Lamb: a title for Jesus. He is compared to a sacrificial lamb in Isaiah 53:7 and appears as a lamb in the book of Revelation.

Lord's Supper: the meal Christians eat together to remember Christ's death. Also called "communion."

Lot: the nephew of Abraham (see Genesis 11:27 – 13:16; 19).

Manna: the "bread" that God miraculously provided each morning for the Israelites to eat while they were journeying to the promised land (see Exodus 16). It looked like white flakes.

Messiah: Christ, the anointed one. In the Old Testament, God promised that the Messiah would come to rescue and rule his people.

Moab: a kingdom in what is now Jordan; the Moabites were traditional enemies of the Israelites.

Omnipotent: all-powerful.

Ordinance: ritual.

Pagan: not knowing or worshiping the true God.

Paradigm: a pattern or model.

Patriarchal: a society ruled by men.

Patriarchs: the "first fathers" of Israel, to whom God gave his promises—Abraham, Isaac, and Jacob.

Pentateuch: the first five books of the Bible—Genesis, Exodus, Leviticus, Numbers, and Deuteronomy.

Piety: doing good deeds for religious reasons.

Post-exilic: the historical period after 538 BC, when Jews returned to Jerusalem and the promised land from exile in Babylon.

Propitiation: appeasing someone's anger at wrongdoing.

Providence: The protective care and power of God, who directs everything for the good of his people.

Quiet time: a common phrase to describe a daily time of prayer and Bible reading.

Rahab: a woman who helped Israelite spies in Jericho and later became part of God's people (see Joshua 2, 6).

Redeemer: someone who restores a close relative's rights or avenges his or her wrongs (see pages 81-83 and 85-92).

Redemption: the act of freeing slaves by paying a cost for them.

Redemptive history: the process throughout history by which God has and will rescue his people from sin to live in relationship with him forever.

Sabbath year: a year of celebration and resting which God told his people to observe every seventh year.

Sacraments: in the Protestant church, the Lord's Supper (communion) and baptism are considered sacraments. Other denominations hold that there are more, and other, "sacraments" (e.g. Roman Catholic "mass").

Saints: a biblical term for all Christians.

Sanctification: the process of becoming more like Christ, by the work of the Holy Spirit.

Satisfaction: paying a debt or fulfilling an obligation.

Social ethic: principles for how to live together in a society.

Sojourner: a foreign resident.

Sovereign: having supreme authority and control.

Systematic Theology: teaching about God and the Bible that is arranged by doctrines in a consistent way.

The creed: a formal statement of Christian belief.

Worldview: the beliefs which we hold in an attempt to make sense of the world as we experience it, and which direct how we live in it. Everyone has a worldview.

Yahweh: the name by which God revealed himself to Moses (Exodus 3:13-14). Literally, it means "I am who I am" or "I will be who I will be". Most English-language Bibles translate it as "Lord".

Zion: another name for Jerusalem (and, more specifically, the mountain upon which it was built).

BIBLIOGRAPHY

- Daniel I. Block, *Judges, Ruth* (B&H, 1999)

- Daniel I. Block, *Ruth: The King Is Coming*, Zondervan Exegetical Commentary on the Old Testament (Zondervan, 2015)

- Iain M. Duguid, *Esther & Ruth*, Reformed Expository Commentary (P&R, 2005)

- Mary J. Evans, *Judges and Ruth*, Tyndale Old Testament Commentaries (IVP USA, 2017)

- Sinclair Ferguson, *Faithful God* (Bryntirion Press, 2013)

- Sidney Greidanus, *Preaching Christ from the Old Testament: A Contemporary Hermeneutical Method* (Eerdmans, 1999)

- Robert L. Hubbard, *The Book of Ruth,* The New International Commentary on the Old Testament (Eerdmans, 1988)

- David Jackman, *Judges/Ruth*, The Preacher's Commentary (Thomas Nelson, 1991)

- Peter H.W. Lau and Gregory Goswell, *Unceasing Kindness*, New Studies in Biblical Theology (IVP USA, 2016)

- Dean R. Ulrich, *From Famine to Fullness* (P&R, 2007)

- K. Lawson Younger Jr., *Judges/Ruth*, The NIV Application Commentary (Zondervan, 2002)

Ruth for Bible-study Groups

Tony Merida's **Good Book Guide** to Ruth is the companion to this resource, helping groups of Christians to explore, discuss and apply the book together. Seven studies, each including investigation, apply, getting personal, pray and explore more sections, take you through the whole of this wonderful narrative. Includes a concise Leader's Guide at the back.

Find out more at:
www.thegoodbook.com/goodbookguides

The God's Word For You Series

- **Exodus For You**
  Tim Chester
- **Judges For You**
  Timothy Keller
- **1 Samuel For You**
  Tim Chester
- **2 Samuel For You**
  Tim Chester
- **Proverbs For You**
  Kathleen Nielson
- **Psalms For You**
  Christopher Ash
- **Daniel For You**
  David Helm
- **Micah For You**
  Stephen Um
- **Luke 1-12 For You**
  Mike McKinley
- **Luke 12-24 For You**
  Mike McKinley
- **John 1-12 For You**
  Josh Moody
- **John 13-21 For You**
  Josh Moody
- **Acts 1-12 For You**
  Albert Mohler

- **Acts 13-28 For You**
  Albert Mohler
- **Romans 1-7 For You**
  Timothy Keller
- **Romans 8-16 For You**
  Timothy Keller
- **2 Corinthians For You**
  Gary Millar
- **Galatians For You**
  Timothy Keller
- **Ephesians For You**
  Richard Coekin
- **Philippians For You**
  Steven Lawson
- **Colossians & Philemon For You**
  Mark Meynell
- **1 & 2 Timothy For You**
  Phillip Jensen
- **Titus For You**
  Tim Chester
- **James For You**
  Sam Allberry
- **1 Peter For You**
  Juan Sanchez
- **Revelation For You**
  Tim Chester

Find out more about these resources at:
www.thegoodbook.com/for-you

BIBLICAL | RELEVANT | ACCESSIBLE

At The Good Book Company, we are dedicated to helping Christians and local churches grow. We believe that God's growth process always starts with hearing clearly what he has said to us through his timeless word—the Bible.

Ever since we opened our doors in 1991, we have been striving to produce Bible-based resources that bring glory to God. We have grown to become an international provider of user-friendly resources to the Christian community, with believers of all backgrounds and denominations using our books, Bible studies, devotionals, evangelistic resources, and DVD-based courses.

We want to equip ordinary Christians to live for Christ day by day, and churches to grow in their knowledge of God, their love for one another, and the effectiveness of their outreach.

Call us for a discussion of your needs or visit one of our local websites for more information on the resources and services we provide.

Your friends at The Good Book Company

thegoodbook.com | thegoodbook.co.uk
thegoodbook.com.au | thegoodbook.co.nz
thegoodbook.co.in